RIVER TROUT FLYFISHING

RIVER TROUT FLYFISHING

PETER LAPSLEY

Illustrations by Graham Gaches

UNWIN

HYMAN

LONDON SYDNEY WELLINGTON

First published in Great Britain by Unwin Hyman, an imprint of
Unwin Hyman Limited, 1988

UNWIN HYMAN LIMITED
15–17 Broadwick Street
London W1V 1FP

Allen & Unwin Australia Pty Ltd
8 Napier Street, North Sydney, NSW 2060, Australia

Allen & Unwin New Zealand Limited with the Port Nicholoson Press,
60 Cambridge Terrace, Wellington, New Zealand

British Library Cataloguing in Publication Data

Lapsley, Peter
  River trout flyfishing.
  1. Trout fishing   2. Flyfishing
  I. Title
  799.1'755   SH687

  ISBN 0–04–440073–X

Set in 11/13pt Bembo Roman by Latimer Trend & Co Ltd
Printed and bound in Great Britain by
Biddles Ltd, Guildford and Kings Lynn

FOREWORD

I know no other book about river trout fishing which gives such clear instruction on the background of fishing, the fish themselves, their habits and food, and all the details of the necessary tackle and techniques for catching them, as this one does. It is a book intended as an introduction to river flyfishing for beginners but it is also an invaluable reference book for those who have already started fishing but are aware how much more they need to know.

I particularly admired Peter Lapsley's long and detailed explanation of how to cast a fly. He gives the best and clearest advice that I have found on this rather complex subject. If you want to find out what the trout are likely to be feeding on in various rivers at various times throughout the country you have only to consult his charts. These are merely two points out of many to admire in a work of distinguished scholarship which will bring you to the heart of the matter, which is, in his words, 'an intimate relationship with rivers'.

CONRAD VOSS BARK
Lifton, Devon

ACKNOWLEDGEMENTS

The production of this book has been a team effort. Several people have given most generously of their time, their expertise and their resources; many more have provided invaluable help and advice.

In particular, my thanks are due to Farlow's of Pall Mall for providing many of the flies for the colour plates and, specifically, to Andrew Witkowski, their manager, for all his assistance; to Hugh Goddard, who processed and printed all my own photographs and who took the colour photographs of the flies; to Ron Holloway, river keeper extraordinary, my guide on the Itchen; to Richard Slocock, the proprietor of Wessex Fly Fishing, for his help with the casting sequences and for his ability to catch trout to order; to Merlin Unwin and Michael Radford for all their patience and advice during the making of the book; and to Conrad Voss Bark for so much kindness over the years and for allowing his name to be formally associated with the completed work.

In addition, I am grateful to John Boyes, Ron Clark, Charles Jardine, Peter Kane, Ian Munroe, Neil Patterson, David Profumo and Anne Voss Bark for their companionship and advice and for so many kind invitations to fish on so many lovely waters during the preparation and writing of the book.

For my wife

LIZA

who gives me the time to fish and to
write, who has provided such enthusiastic
and unstinting support while I have been
working on this book and who took more
than half of the photographs for it.

CONTENTS

ILLUSTRATIONS

Line drawings

PREFACE

Between Beroea and Thessalonica there flows a river called the Astaeus. Now there are in it fishes of a speckled hue, but what the natives call them, it is better to enquire of the Macedonians. Now these fish feed upon the flies of the country which flit about the river and which are quite unlike flies elsewhere . . . the natives call them Hippurus. These flies settle on the stream and seek the food that they like; they cannot however escape the observations of the fishes that swim below.

So when a fish observes a Hippurus on the surface it swims up noiselessly under water for fear of disturbing the surface and to avoid scaring its prey. Then when close at hand in the fly's shadow it opens its jaws and swallows the fly, just as a wolf snatches a sheep from the flock, or as an eagle seizes a goose from the farmyard. Having done this it plunges beneath the ripple.

Now although fishermen know of these happenings, they do not in fact make any use of these flies as baits for fish, because if the human hand touches them it destroys the natural bloom; their wings wither and the fish refuse to eat them, and for that reason will not go near them because by some mysterious instinct they detest flies that have been caught.

And so with the skill of anglers the men circumvent the fish by the following artful contrivance. They wrap the hook in scarlet wool, and to the wool they attach two feathers that grow beneath a cock's wattles and are the colour of wax. The fishing rod is six feet long, and so is the line. So they let down this lure, and the fish being attracted and excited by the colour, comes to meet it, and fancying from the beauty of the sight that he is going to have a wonderful banquet, opens wide his mouth, is entangled with the hook, and gains a bitter feast, for he is caught.

Aelian (AD *c.* 170–235)
From *De Natura Animalium*, Book XV, Chapter 1,
translated from the Greek by A. E. Schofield

INTRODUCTION

People have been fishing with flies in Britain at least since the end of the fifteenth century and possibly since much earlier than that, but it is only in the past hundred years or so that flyfishing has moved away from the rest of freshwater angling and become surrounded by a mystique and jargon all of its own. Today, angling is said to be the most popular participant pastime in the country, with some $3\frac{1}{2}$ million people going in pursuit of coarse, game or sea fish every year. Of these, a substantial number fish chiefly or exclusively for trout.

Angling pressure on our streams and rivers has increased several hundredfold since the middle of the last century, and lakes, gravel pits and reservoirs have been pressed into service to meet the growing demand for trout fishing. This has given rise to a new breed of angler – the stillwater flyfisher – and has led to the development of a whole new range of tackle and techniques. I have done a great deal of stillwater trouting myself and would not deny for one moment that it is a fascinating and challenging pursuit. But, like many others, I find myself constantly drawn back to running water. Whether on a declining Home Counties river like the Chess, where I cast my first fly more than thirty years ago, on a tumbling Cumbrian beck, on a spate river pouring from Dartmoor, on a great salmon river in Scotland, on one of the larger and more fertile rivers that run down from the Pennines, or amongst the tranquillity of the water meadows through which flow the chalk streams of southern England, it is on running water that the spirit and the soul of flyfishing are to be found.

It is possible to develop a much more intimate relationship with a river than with a stillwater. Given time and patience, we can get to know every pool, stickle, curve and weed bed, every undercut bank and overhanging tree; we can learn to predict changes in its mood and in the moods of the fish; and we can see and study the flies upon which the trout feed. We can develop an empathy with the birds and animals that inhabit the bankside vegetation – mallard and kingfishers, moorhens and water voles and the myriad other creatures that show themselves only to those who spend time at the waterside 'studying to be quiet'.

We can develop an affinity, too, with the valley through which a river flows, with the wildlife it sustains, with its trees and flowers, with the cows, bullocks, sheep and horses that graze it, and with the farms and hamlets that have been built in it. A river valley is almost always a self-contained community in its own right, with its own character, its own clearly defined geography and its own communications, all focused upon the river. It will also often have a womb-like quality; confined by the hills that rise on either side, the cares of the world are distanced from us. The next valley over can become remote; the towns or cities in which we may live can seem a million miles away.

There is a myth that river trout fishing has become too expensive and too inaccessible for all but the wealthy. Nothing could be further from the truth. Even on the lovely chalk streams of densely populated south-eastern England, where the demand for fishing is at its heaviest, there are substantial stretches of good water owned or leased by angling clubs which anyone can join for quite modest subscriptions. In addition, there are day-ticket stretches on several of the best chalk streams, and I know of several syndicates that have taken leases at very reasonable cost on a number of delightful brooks in Hampshire, Wiltshire and Dorset.

Further afield – as one moves away from the main centres of population – there is wonderful fishing to be had on spate rivers in Devon and Cornwall, Wales, the north of England, Scotland and Northern Ireland, if not for the asking, at least for the payment of a small fee. Some of these waters are owned by hotels which issue tickets both to residents and to non-residents; others are in the hands of clubs and associations which visitors can join on a temporary basis.

Even for those who choose to fish private, carefully keepered rivers in, say, Yorkshire or the south of England, the cost of a rod is likely to be reasonable when compared with the price of a gun on a shoot or even with membership of a respectable golf club.

So there is really no reason why those who wish to fish for trout in streams and rivers should not be able to do so, either regularly, throughout the season, or occasionally, on holidays or when kind friends offer a day or so on their waters.

Which brings us to the purpose of this book, written for newcomers to river flyfishing, both complete beginners and those who may only have fished stillwaters before, for those who have fished but one kind of stream or river and wish to try others, and for those who have been fishing for some time and wish to increase their understanding of the sport and to improve their techniques.

It would be impertinent of me – as it would of any fishing writer – to try to tell other anglers what they should seek from their sport. Personally, I do not subscribe to the view that a blank day should be just as enjoyable as one on which we start the homeward trek with a heavy creel. Nor do I believe that enjoyment of a day spent at the waterside can be measured solely by the weight of one's catch. There is, in the words of The Flyfishers' Club motto, a good deal more to fishing than just catching fish.

Flyfishing as a whole, and river flyfishing in particular, is a very traditional pursuit. Successive generations have inherited knowledge and understanding from their forebears, retaining equipment, techniques and standards that seem valid and only cautiously discarding those that do not. I believe that an understanding of the background to our sport can do much to enhance our enjoyment of it. I have therefore included a chapter on the history of river flyfishing and one exploring its present state and its future in the hope that they may whet people's appetites, encouraging them to explore some of the works listed as 'Background Material' in the bibliography.

I also believe that we can increase both our enjoyment of river flyfishing and our success in it by developing an understanding of the characteristics of the streams we fish, of the trout themselves and of the creatures they live on. For this reason, I have included reasonably detailed exposés on all three subjects.

But, above all, I believe that we go fishing chiefly to catch fish. So my essential purpose in writing this book is to explain the tackle, techniques and tactics that are required for the reasonably consistent taking of trout from running waters.

Note that I say 'explain' rather than 'teach'. Nobody can be taught to fish solely through the printed word. Crafts and manual skills can only be taught by explanation, demonstration and practice. Flyfishing is no exception. I hope that this book may go some way towards meeting the first of these requirements. But I would most strongly suggest that the beginner should build upon what he or she may have assimilated from it by going to a qualified instructor, particularly in order to learn to cast. Without at least a modicum of casting ability, flyfishing – and especially river flyfishing, which demands quite high standards of accuracy and delicacy – is likely to be little more than an exercise in rarefied frustration.

Two organizations in the United Kingdom examine would-be game angling instructors and certify their competence – The Association of Professional Game Angling Instructors and The National Anglers' Council.

Both will willingly direct you towards conveniently located representatives, and the addresses of both are given in Appendix IV at the end of this book.

Those who count themselves specialists – whether, for example, with the dry fly on southern chalk streams, with the upstream wet fly on northern spate rivers or with traditional attractor patterns on sea-trout waters in Wales or in the West Country – may be concerned by the egalitarianism of my approach to stream and river fishing. I make no apology for it. Over the years, I have become increasingly convinced that trout behave in very much the same ways wherever they are to be found and it is we, rather than they, who have brought about the variations in styles of fishing now to be found throughout the country. I believe that an understanding of all the major techniques can improve our ability to take trout from any stream or river, and that our choice of tackle and tactics should be governed chiefly by pragmatism (leavened with strict adherence to the rules of the fishery), rather than solely by local custom.

The parameters within which this work is written are, inevitably, somewhat arbitrary. Anybody who fishes for trout on streams and rivers for any length of time will, eventually and almost inevitably, find himself on waters inhabited by grayling and sea trout. So similar are these fish to brown and rainbow trout in their habits, and so closely related to those used for trout are the techniques employed in their capture, that it seems prudent to include a chapter on each of these species. But to do so presents me with a problem.

Particularly in the north of England, it is perfectly acceptable to fish for grayling with worms, just as upstream worming for trout is a wholly acceptable (and extremely skilful) technique in parts of Ireland, Scotland, Wales and the West Country. But I have never wormed for trout or grayling myself, and it seems to me quite wrong to hold forth upon a style of fishing about which I know very little. So this is a book about flyfishing.

Finally, I would not suggest, nor would I wish anyone to believe, that this is in any way a definitive work on river flyfishing. Ours is too complex a pursuit, with too many subtle differences in types of water and too many variations of local tradition and practice, to be covered in any single volume. But I hope that the book may help to strip away some of the mumbo-jumbo and mystique that has been built up around the sport and that it may provide a sound framework of knowledge upon which the reader may be able to build through his or her experience and experimentation, perhaps leavened with sound advice from other anglers. If it achieves this purpose, I shall be well satisfied.

PETER LAPSLEY
July 1987

1
THE
LEGACY OF
THE PAST

Nobody seems to be quite sure how long people have been flyfishing for trout in Britain's streams and rivers. Very little was written about anything, let alone about angling, before the end of the fifteenth century.

The first references to flyfishing here are to be found in Dame Juliana Berners's *Treatyse of Fysshinge with an Angle*, published in 1496 as an appendix to her *Book of St Albans*, a manual on hawking, hunting and heraldry.

There has been much debate as to who Dame Juliana was (allegedly the Prioress of Sopwell), whether she actually wrote the book (quite possibly not), where it was actually printed and published (probably on a press within the grounds of Westminster Abbey) and when it was really written. Only the last point is of any serious consequence. The *Treatyse* clearly refers to flyfishing as an established practice. If, as has been suggested, it was actually committed to paper some fifty years earlier than the imprint date, then we may safely presume that people have been flyfishing for trout,

5

salmon, grayling and dace (the species described by Berners) for sport – rather than simply as a means of obtaining food – at least since the middle of the fifteenth century.

The tackle of the times, quite comprehensively described in the *Treatyse*, was homespun and must have required as much skill in its manufacture as in its use. Rods, from thirteen to fourteen feet long, were of three pieces, with butts of blackthorn or medlar, middle sections of willow, hazel or ash, and tips of hazel. The upper ends of the butt and middle sections were made hollow with a red-hot spike to form female ferrules into which the next pieces were fitted. The angler made his own hooks from square-headed needles, shaping them, cutting the barbs, flattening the ends and retempering them before whipping them to spun, tapered, knotted horsehair lines, anything from two to six strands thick at the point, marginally longer than the rods and attached to loops at the rod tips.

Berners described the dressings for a dozen artificial flies, using wool of various colours for the bodies and partridge, drake and buzzard feathers, and red cock hackles, as wings. Her flies do not appear to have been dressed with collar, beard or palmered hackles as ours are, and the woollen bodies will quickly have become waterlogged, but she clearly understood at least the principles of dry-fly fishing, advocating the use of artificial flies when fish were rising.

But, if pragmatism is the opposite of purism in piscatorial terms, Berners was an avowedly pragmatic angler, as content to fish for trout with caterpillars, worms, dapped natural flies or minnows as with dressed fly patterns, and to fish for pike, perch, roach, bream and dace as happily as for trout. This was to be a guiding philosophy for most anglers for the next 350 years.

Izaac Walton, who first published his pastorally delightful but less than instructive work *The Compleat Angler* in 1653, was more of a bait fisher than a flyfisher, but his angling companion, Charles Cotton, who contributed an appendix to the fifth edition of the book, was essentially a flyfisher. A Derbyshire country squire, he fished the Dove for trout as a boy on his father's property at Beresford Hall on Derbyshire's border with Staffordshire and later with Walton (his senior by some 37 years) when he had inherited the estate.

For all that their tackle may seem rudimentary today, it should not be thought that those who fished or wrote about fishing during the fifteenth, sixteenth and seventeenth centuries were unsophisticated. Indeed, Berners, Walton and Cotton all taught lessons too often ignored by modern anglers – dress unobtrusively; keep out of sight; match tackle and tactics to the season, the state of the water and the behaviour of the fish; and fish as light as you sensibly can.

Tackle developed but slowly during the seventeenth and eighteenth centuries. Reels, invented by the Chinese in the twelfth century, eventually came into use in Europe in the middle of the seventeenth century, but they seem to have been slow in becoming widely accepted, with people persevering both with lines fastened directly to their rod tips and with a variety of running line contrivances – bobbins, frames not unlike those used for sea fishing hand-lines today, cleats and, the simplest of all expedients, the gathering of the line in the hand or on the ground.

Rods remained almost unchanged well into the nineteenth century. Certainly, they became longer (Cotton recommended one fifteen to eighteen feet long) and whole cane and whalebone were introduced – the former for middle joints and the latter to act as shock absorbers at the tip. But the principles of their construction and use were constant (and approximated closely to those we see in roach poles still used by many coarse anglers today).

In the middle of the sixteenth century, catgut and (slightly later) silkworm thread became known as possible alternatives to the length or two of horsehairs nearest to the fly. But, although gut was stronger than horsehair, could be drawn finer and was less visible, it was scarcer, more difficult to tie secure knots with and was found to rot more quickly, so relatively few people used it. Similarly, lines made of silk had been experimented with by the second half of the seventeenth century but failed to find widespread favour – probably because of the ease with which they tangled – and spun knotted tapered horsehair remained in general use well into the nineteenth century.

Dame Juliana's twelve fly patterns burgeoned into some sixty-five listed by Cotton in his appendix to *The Compleat Angler* and continued to multiply at an extraordinary rate over the years thereafter. The vast majority of seventeenth- and eighteenth-century patterns were intended by those who dressed them to imitate or represent natural flies seen on the water. It was not really until the nineteenth century that attractor patterns began to come into their own – chiefly for sea trout but also for loch and river fishing for brown trout.

The predisposition towards the use of imitative patterns was reflected in the ways in which they were fished. There is some evidence to suggest that, rather than simply floating them on the surface until they became waterlogged and then being content to allow them to sink beneath it, anglers were increasingly and calculatedly fishing dry flies to trout that were rising and wet ones to those that were not. In his *Vade Mecum of Fly Fishing for Trout*, first published in 1841, G. R. P. Pulman described dry-fly fishing thus:

If the wet and heavy fly be exchanged for a dry and light one, and passed in artistic style over the feeding fish, it will, partly from the simple circumstances of its buoyancy, be taken, in nine cases out of ten, as greedily as the living insect itself.

Thus Pulman seems to have been the father of dry-fly fishing as we understand it today, but the choice between dry and wet fly was still heavily subject to the limitations of tackle and to the dictates of the wind.

After almost three hundred years of near stagnation in terms of tackle design, the middle of the nineteenth century saw spectacular advances suddenly being made. Greenheart replaced blackthorn, ash, hazel and whole bamboo for rod manufacture, and was itself quickly replaced with built cane. And dressed silk lines – tapered, heavier and far less prone to tangling than anything that had gone before – became available, as did eyed hooks, known to anglers almost since time immemorial but not available in suitable forms for fly dressing until about 1880.

The growth of the dry-fly cult in the latter half of the nineteenth century was almost certainly a direct consequence of these three major innovations. Drag – the skidding of a fly on the water's surface, caused by tension on fly line and leader – however slight, is the greatest technical problem faced by the dry-fly fisher, and can only be overcome by casting upstream. The combination of the new, stiffer rods and heavier, more manageable lines freed flyfishers from the dictates of the wind, enabling them to cast across it or even into it – which allowed them to cast upstream as and when they wished, rather than merely when the wind decreed that they should.

However good the floatants available, artificial flies eventually become waterlogged and sink, especially if they are taken by fish. The eyed hook made it possible to change flies quickly and easily, which overcame this problem.

So, quite suddenly, dry-fly fishing became an entirely practical proposition. Not surprisingly, flyfishers pursued the new and exciting technique with great energy and enthusiasm, particularly on the chalk streams of southern England. The enthusiasm was fuelled by the writings of several extremely articulate angling authors, F. M. Halford – the high priest of the art – being foremost amongst them. They argued (quite wrongly, as we shall see in due course) that chalk-stream trout lived almost exclusively on winged adult flies, and they made a cult of the dry fly. So widely accepted were their preachings that by the beginning of the twentieth century it had become generally believed that to take trout by any other means was in some way unsporting, and 'dry fly only' had become the accepted rule on most chalk-stream fisheries.

It has become fashionable to cast Halford in some way as the villain of the piece in the development of dry-fly purism. In fairness, he was not. He was a highly perceptive and imaginative angler with more than a touch of pragmatism in his philosophy towards his sport. As is so often the case with any cult, it was Halford's disciples – those who took his teachings as gospel, without questioning or analysing them and without leavening them with common sense – who did the damage. And much damage they did.

Hitherto, anglers had been anglers in the broadest sense of that word. No doubt some had preferred flyfishing to legering or legering to float fishing, but the division between what we now call game and coarse fishing had been an ill defined one. (The records of the Amwell Magna Fishery, one of the oldest in the country, clearly show that members pursued pike, perch, roach and chub in preference to trout right up to the early 1900s.)

The advances in fly tackle quite suddenly created a clear division between coarse and game anglers, and the growth of dry-fly purism further divided game anglers into those who fished the chalk streams and those who fished elsewhere. It also gave flyfishing an elitist, holier-than-thou image throughout the angling community and amongst the public at large. Worse than all this though, it stultified the imaginations of those who fished the chalk streams and inhibited intelligent experimentation and progress. So entrenched did the views of the chalk-stream pundits become that they are still reflected in the rules of some fisheries today, despite the work done by people like G. E. M. Skues, Frank Sawyer and Sawyer's own disciple, Oliver Kite, who pointed to the fallacies upon which dry-fly purism was based and established and promoted nymph fishing as an acceptable alternative to it.

While the chalk-stream anglers were going their own esoteric way during the late nineteenth century, flyfishers in other parts of the United Kingdom were developing and refining their own styles and techniques. In the borders and in the north of England, perhaps the most skilful of all fly-fishing methods, the upstream wet fly, was being perfected, with tiny, delicate spider patterns, often in teams of two or three, being cast upstream on short lines. On spate rivers in Wales, north-west England and in Scotland, fancy patterns were coming into their own, fished across and downstream, very often for sea trout at night. And, in the south-west of England – in Devon and Cornwall – and on the great rivers of eastern Scotland, those who were not engaged in the pursuit of salmon fished pragmatically for trout and sea trout, borrowing dry-fly techniques from the chalk-stream flyfishers, using upstream wet flies as they saw fit and fishing across and down with attractor patterns, chiefly for sea trout at night.

The first serious assault on chalk-stream elitism came from G. E. M. Skues, a skilled and observant angler and an immensely literate and articulate lawyer. He noted that, when they were not rising to winged adult flies floating on the surface, chalk-stream trout could often be found to be feeding below the surface on the nymphs ascending through the water to hatch. He devised a series of patterns to represent the nymphs, developed a technique for fishing them and publicized his successes in a series of erudite and readable books and articles.

This challenge to those who made a fetish out of the 'precise imitation' of winged adult flies, and of only ever fishing a dry fly upstream to seen, feeding fish, caused an enormous stir in the angling world, culminating in a brief, heated and now famous debate at The Flyfishers' Club in London in 1938. With great wit and sharpness, Skues exposed the irrationality and illogicality of the purists' arguments for the humbug they were. This was an important victory. It marked a turning-point after some thirty or forty years of stultification of thought on the chalk streams, and it was followed by gradual, if sometimes grudging, acceptance of the validity of the nymph as an alternative to the dry fly.

Shortly before his death, Skues's educational work was taken up by another man of an entirely different kind. Frank Sawyer was the river keeper on the Services' Dry Fly Fishing Association water on the upper Avon in Wiltshire for over fifty years, from 1928 until his death in 1980. Sawyer was an exceptional naturalist and a skilful and innovative flyfisher. He also became an accomplished broadcaster and writer, so his observations and techniques received a good deal of publicity.

Whereas Skues had produced a whole range of nymphs designed to imitate the naturals, Sawyer relied on just two – the Pheasant Tail Nymph and the Grey Goose Nymph – as generally representative patterns. And he caused a certain amount of consternation amongst the chalk stream traditionalists by weighting them with wire. But so obviously perceptive and knowledgeable was Sawyer, and so firmly had the validity of nymph fishing become established by Skues's work, that the carping was short-lived and most river flyfishers embraced his teachings enthusiastically.

It should not be thought that Skues, Sawyer or their adherents were renegades, cocking a snook at established practice out of devilment. They were, in fact, expert entomologists, astute observers of life in, on and around the water and highly accomplished dry-fly fishers. Their essential talent, though, was that they were able to cut through the humbug and mystique that had been built up around the sport, to open people's eyes to the realities of the trout's behaviour and feeding habits and to broaden anglers' horizons, making chalk-stream flyfishing a markedly more interesting and challenging pursuit.

The eyes they opened were those of growing numbers of increasingly mobile flyfishers vying for places on decreasing numbers of streams and rivers.

The arrival of the train and subsequently the motor car, combined with increasing affluence and leisure time, led to a dramatic growth in angling pressure on waters of all sorts, and trout streams were no exception. Whereas hitherto dons and undergraduates from Oxford had made something of an expedition of riding out to Fairford to spend a weekend fishing the Colne, now, quite suddenly, individuals and groups of flyfishers could board a train at Waterloo on a Saturday morning, be on the water on the Itchen by ten, and be back in London by bedtime having fished the evening rise. And similar excursions were becoming increasingly practicable throughout the United Kingdom.

But if this revolution increased people's ability to go fishing, it did nothing to enhance the variety and quality of the country's trout streams. Urban sprawl engulfed many pretty and productive rivers, especially in the Home Counties. Pollution from factories built exclusively with economic, rather than environmental, considerations in mind poisoned and de-oxygenated many more. And abstraction of water for industrial and domestic purposes, both from the water tables and directly from the rivers themselves, reduced many watercourses to mere shadows of their former selves.

This stretching of the supply-and-demand equation has been resolved – albeit on an *ad hoc* basis, rather than through some grand scheme – by limiting access to rivers, by increasing the capacity of the rivers themselves to accommodate anglers and by turning increasing numbers of stillwaters into trout fisheries to cater for the overflow.

A long-established tradition of riparian ownership, especially in England, provided the key to limitation of access. As more and more people began to seek fishing, so increasingly did proprietors of stretches of water begin to recognize the value of their assets and to lease them to syndicates or clubs. Inevitably, prices rose, particularly on good water in densely populated areas, and very soon the cost of fishing a chalk stream in southern England had outstripped most anglers' pockets. Elsewhere, most notably in Scotland and Ireland, but also in Wales and in the north and west of England, where fishing pressure has been lighter than in the south-east, the gap between supply and demand has remained narrower, so access has been less restricted and the cost of fishing has been held at more modest levels.

These differences between lightly and heavily populated areas are also reflected in an interesting geographical coincidence.

Rivers around London, and especially those to the south and west of the capital, generally rise in chalk downlands and tend to fluctuate little in level, to be clear and to be remarkably fertile. These characteristics produce water perfect for flyfishing in which the trout grow fit and fat. Inevitably, more people would like to be able to fish such waters than can actually do so.

In contrast, most of the other rivers in our islands rise on hills or moorland, can vary quite dramatically in level, may quite often be coloured and tend to be relatively infertile (notwithstanding Driffield Beck and the limestone rivers of Derbyshire and northern Cumbria). But that is not to say that the fishing on them is any less exciting or rewarding.

The reasons for these differences in the natures of our rivers, and the effects those differences have on the fish and the fishing, will be considered in detail in the chapter that follows.

2

THE RIVERS

AND THEIR FISH

In the simplest terms, the nature and characteristics of any stream or river are governed by the nature of the land over or through which its water flows, and the species and quality of the fish it sustains are governed by the nature and characteristics of the river. Small, infertile streams support small trout (or no fish at all); larger, more fertile and well oxygenated rivers support larger trout and, quite often, grayling, dace, chub and pike; and, in their lower reaches, where they are sluggish, less well aerated and often prone to silting, rivers usually support coarse fish, rather than trout.

Almost all streams and rivers of any size change in character between their sources and their estuaries or the points at which they join other watercourses. Most obviously, the speed of the water drops and the size of a stream grows as the valley through which it flows flattens out and tributaries join it. But other, more complicated, factors have roles to play, too.

As water runs through or over rock, it absorbs dissolved mineral salts which fertilize it. The softer the rock, the more easily is it dissolved, particularly if the water spends a substantial period of time in contact with it. Chalk and, to a lesser extent, sandstone and limestone are soft and readily dissolved; granite is hard and yields almost no salts at all – which is why

13

chalk and limestone streams produce luxuriant weed growth and big trout, while rivers running off granite mountains produce little weed and small trout.

The vegetation in the water catchment areas can also significantly influence the nature of a stream. Where rainwater seeps into a watercourse through peat or through decaying bracken, heather or pine needles, the stream will usually have a brown tinge, often quite dark (which excludes light and thus inhibits weed growth), and its water will be acid.

Man, that inveterate meddler, has also altered the characters of most of our rivers. In many areas, chemical fertilizers used for agricultural purposes are washed off the land or leach through it, significantly increasing the fertility of some rivers, often to their detriment. Weed choking a watercourse benefits neither fish nor fisherman.

Some rivers have been dammed to form reservoirs from which water is drawn for domestic and industrial consumption. Such abstraction drastically reduces water levels below the dams, occasionally to the extent that near-dry stream beds have to be flushed through by regular, controlled release of water from the reservoirs. And, of course, dams of any sort can obstruct the passage of migratory fish. Even where fish passes have been built, the runs of salmon and sea trout are almost always smaller than they were before man's interference.

In the middle and lower reaches of many rivers, 'improved' land drainage has sharply increased the speed at which water levels rise and fall in response to rainfall. In contrast, relief channels designed to carry flood water away now contain the excesses of a few rivers, reducing the levels to which they rise and helping to prevent them from breaking their banks. And draconian dredging and weed cutting, done solely to improve drainage, can both turn attractive and productive streams into dull, lifeless canals.

And, lastly, man, of course, has developed an astonishing array of techniques for polluting rivers – from sewage and industrial and chemical effluent through the seepage of agricultural waste to run-off from dirty, oily roads and the accidental spillage of petrol, oil, creosote, and so on. Pollution de-oxygenates the water, killing fish and other animal life by suffocation, sometimes for very considerable distances downstream. In the worst cases, once-lovely trout streams have been bled almost dry by abstraction and then simply poisoned with all manner of waste until they have become nothing more than noxious and unsightly open sewers.

But the purpose of this chapter is to examine the many marvellous rivers that remain, rather than to bemoan those that have gone, and not all of the work done by man has been detrimental. Indeed, some – especially on the chalk streams, but on some other waters too – has greatly benefited the fish and, therefore, the angler. Hatches and weirs, usually built for purposes other than simply to improve a fishery, oxygenate the water and encourage it to carve out deep pools, providing ideal holding areas for trout and grayling. And bridges provide shade and shelter, often otherwise lacking on some streams, which is why it always pays to approach them cautiously and fish them carefully.

The essential difference between a chalk stream or brook and other burns, becks and rivers lies in their respective sources and in the nature of the land over which they flow.

CHALK STREAMS

Chalk is highly permeable and rain falling onto it soaks straight into it, as into a sponge, rather than simply running off it. As the water sinks down through the chalk it is filtered and then settles into the water table or aquifer. In section, the aquifer is domed, rather than having a flat surface like a lake. The dome rises and falls through the year in response to rainfall, being at its highest in early spring, after the winter's downpours, and at its lowest towards the end of the summer. Throughout its time in the aquifer, the water is absorbing salts from the chalk and becoming increasingly fertile.

As the dome rises, its edge reaches points of weakness in the ground and the water pours out, running away as a stream. Not unnaturally, the springs lowest in the water table are the earliest to break and the last to fail. Some, below the point to which the top of the water table never falls, never fail. Others, high up, break late and always fail by July or August. Streams fed by such predictably fallible springs are termed 'winterbournes'.

Rivers fed by chalk springs make ideal trout fisheries. Their water is clear, which enables us to see the fish. They rise and fall very little in response to rain because the water tends to soak into the chalk, rather than run straight off it, which means that the rivers remain fishable almost regardless of the weather. And they are extremely fertile and therefore sustain large quantities of weed, which in turn sustains a vast wealth of insect life, which in turn produces big, healthy fish – and some problems.

Weed cutting is hard work for river keepers, and to cut weed properly is a considerable craft. The objects are to provide open lies for the fish and fishable water for the fisherman, and to maintain the flow of the water while at the same time leaving sufficient weed to provide prolific larders for the trout. It is also important that damaging weed like starwort, which encourages silting, should be removed and that good weeds like ranunculus and water celery, which provide excellent shelter for the creatures trout eat and do not accumulate mud, should just be given judicious haircuts.

Weed cutting is hard work for river keepers. On major chalk streams like the Itchen, weed cutting dates are agreed so that the damage to fishing is kept to a minimum.

On major chalk streams like the Test, the Itchen, the Kennet and the Wylye, and the Driffield Beck in Yorkshire, the river keepers agree weed-cutting dates before the season opens and all cut their weed at the same time. With great rafts of weed floating down on their currents, the rivers are effectively unfishable on weed-cutting days and for a day or so thereafter, and a well publicized programme enables anglers to avoid the irritation thus caused. On small chalk brooks, like the Ebble and the Piddle, it is usually possible to run a net from bank to bank, cut a stretch immediately upstream of it and then haul the weed out. This obviates the need for a co-ordinated programme on those rivers where the job is usually done by busy riparian owners, rather than by full-time professional keepers.

SPATE RIVERS

Spate rivers are far more variable in character than chalk streams, the quality of their water being a direct product of the ground on which they rise and over which they run, but they all have one thing in common. Although some are augmented by springs or lakes, they are all either largely or exclusively fed by rainwater running off the land. As a

16

consequence, they tend to rise and fall very quickly in response to rainfall or the lack of it, and they tend to be innately infertile because the bedrock is hard, containing few soluble mineral salts, and because they are in direct contact with it only relatively briefly.

The rapid rise and fall of a spate river is significant. When the water is low, its banks and the beds of the streams and rivulets feeding it dry out and accumulate an assortment of wind-borne bits and pieces – leaves, twigs, dust and loose soil. When the rain comes, it washes all this material down the watercourse, and the river becomes coloured and, usually, unfishable.

Spates can also be hazardous to anglers, rivers rising very rapidly with little or no warning. The fisherman wading on midstream shallows which may have been readily accessible when the water was low can find himself cut off from the bank surprisingly easily, and a few flyfishers are actually swept away by flash floods each year.

I myself have been alarmed on occasions. I was fishing the Eden below Appleby one fine June evening a few years ago. The sky was lightly overcast, but there was no sign of rain. Just before dusk, with no warning at all, the river rose more than two feet in less than twenty minutes, presumably in response to a storm high in the Pennines an hour or so earlier. I made it to the bank but acquired a pair of very soggy socks in the process.

FERTILITY

The fertility of a stream or river – or its lack – is important to the angler too, not only because it has a direct (and predictable) effect on the species and sizes of the fish that live in it and the varieties and quantities of the creatures they live on, but also because it influences the behaviour of the trout and the ways in which they feed. At opposite ends of the scale, in a chalk stream or in a fertile spate river such as the Eden, luxuriant weed beds may be found across the whole width of the river. The trout take up lies amongst them and in the gaps between them, which means that they may be found almost anywhere. And, with a mass of food to choose from, they can afford to be selective and often are. In contrast, infertile streams, like the headwaters of most spate rivers and major rivers such as the Teign in Devonshire and the Swale in Yorkshire, are sparse in weed. The trout that live in them take up lies wherever they can find refuge from the current, shade in summer and protection from predators – ahead of and behind rocks and boulders, by groynes and fallen branches, under overhanging trees and bushes and in the slack water beneath steep, cut-away banks. And, with food in short supply, they are very often free-rising and relatively unselective.

17

THE QUARRY

And so we come to the fish themselves. Those that inhabit British rivers and may be taken on artificial flies are brown trout, sea trout, grayling, chub, dace, and rainbow trout. All but the rainbow, an import from the United States and now reared in almost all trout farms here, are indigenous. In heavily fished rivers, wild brown trout have to share the water with farm-reared ones, but the grayling, chub and dace are all wild (although grayling have only relatively recently been introduced into some rivers – the Eden is an example).

All of these fish have certain characteristics in common, especially in terms of feeding, eyesight and their senses of hearing, smell and taste, so I shall consider our primary quarry, the brown trout, in detail and then examine the other species by comparing them with it.

THE BROWN TROUT (*Salmon trutta*)

Brown trout, found in every trout stream and river throughout the British Isles, are the perfect quarry for the flyfisher. They vary enormously in both size and appearance according to the type of water they inhabit – from the great, deep, bronze and often lightly marked aldermen of the Test and

A wild brown trout from the Wylye; the bread and butter quarry of most river flyfishers.

Itchen, occasionally weighing three or four pounds or even more, through the bright, light golden, black-and-vermilion-spotted three-quarter-pounders of the Exe and the Eden, to the fierce, dark and slender three- or four-ounce fish of the Deveron and the Upper Bann.

LIFE-CYCLE

Brown trout spawn in the winter, between the beginning of December and mid- to late February. In order to do so, they move into stretches of river with clean gravel beds through which the water can percolate, washing the eggs. These areas, known as redds, are often upstream of the trouts' spring, summer and autumn haunts.

On a redd, a hen fish cuts a hollow in the gravel with sweeps of her tail and then lays some of the several hundred ova she is carrying into it. Simultaneously, her mate, holding position beside and usually very slightly ahead of her, discharges a stream of milt into the current, some of it reaching and fertilizing the ova. The hen fish then moves a foot or so upstream and cuts another hollow, the pebbles washed out of it covering the fertilized ova in the previous one and thus protecting them.

Mating, although not usually fatal, is a debilitating process for trout, and they may need as much as two or three months to regain condition, which is why the trout season is generally closed from the end of October until the middle of April (although the opening date is extremely variable, ranging from the middle of January on some Scottish rivers to the beginning of May on one or two chalk streams). Especially in rivers sparse in food, a few of the older fish may be unable to compete with the younger ones and fail altogether to put back weight lost in spawning. Such trout, readily identifiable by their gauntness, even when caught in June or July, are best compassionately dispatched, although they will be unfit for all but the least fastidious of tastes.

After about four to twelve weeks in the redds (depending on the water temperature), the trout's ova hatch into alevins, strange, almost tadpole-like creatures which continue to live for some time on yolk sacs hanging from their throats. As the yolk sacs become depleted, the alevins become increasingly fish-like and are soon clearly identifiable as trout fry.

The fry live in shoals in slack water, usually close to the shore, and feed on the minute invertebrates they find there. They, in turn, provide easy pickings for a whole range of predators and the mortality rate from the oval stage until the young trout are big enough to be reasonably safe is staggeringly high. Even when fully grown, trout continue to be preyed upon by herons, otters, mink and pike, although there is some evidence to suggest that when less agile coarse fish are present the major predators (man excluded) will take them in preference to the trout.

19

In ideal conditions, brown trout may live for anything from eight to twelve years, becoming sexually mature in their fourth year. They are essentially individualistic, adopting lies which provide them with refuge from the full force of the stream and cover from predators and strong direct sunlight, but where they can still take full advantage of the conveyor belt of food borne down to them on the current. Brown trout do not normally move far from their lies to intercept food, rarely more than about three feet. Each one has its own identified bolt-hole, usually quite close to its lie, into which it will slip if it believes danger to threaten.

There is a clearly established pecking order amongst brown trout in streams and rivers, the biggest and fittest fish almost always occupying the best lies. And, when a fish is caught or otherwise evicted from his lie, it is remarkable how often it will quickly be taken over by another trout.

FEEDING

There is a myth, probably started by the chalk-stream pundits of the late nineteenth century, that trout, particularly chalk-stream trout, live exclusively on genteel diets of mayflies, pale wateries and iron blue duns. Nothing could be further from the truth. Trout are simply carnivorous predators, feeding on any living creature small enough, palatable enough and accessible enough for them to eat.

It is, of course, impossible to quantify the proportions of their food that trout take from the surface or beneath it; the figures vary widely from water to water. But I am quite certain that on most rivers, and especially on the most fertile ones, substantially more than 50 per cent – and quite possibly as much as 85 per cent – is taken from well below the surface.

The trout's chief objective in life is to acquire enough protein to enable it to thrive and grow, and to do this with the least possible expenditure of effort. To this end, it will take nymphs and sedge and stonefly larvae from the stream or river bed, snails, nymphs and freshwater shrimps from amongst the weed, fry of all sorts from the marginal shallows and terrestrial insects – gnats, hawthorn flies, caterpillars, beetles, daddy-long-legs and moths – which fall or are blown onto the water from overhanging trees and bushes and from surrounding fields and hedgerows, just as cheerfully as they will take nymphs ascending to hatch and adult upwinged flies and sedges.

The fishes' feeding habits are chiefly dictated by the temperature of the water and by the availability of food. Brown trout will feed when the water temperature is between 8° and 15°C and do so most enthusiastically when it is between 10° and 13°C. (They can survive in water between about 0° and 20°C provided it is sufficiently well oxygenated, but become increasingly torpid as the temperature approaches either of these extremes.)

Early in the season, when the water is cold, the fish tend to stay close to the bottom and to feed, when they do so at all, on such food forms as may be available to them there. As both the water and the air warm up through April, May and early June, the trout will take advantage of the increasing variety of insects available to them, culminating on some rivers, especially in Ireland and in the south of England, with the mayfly hatch which runs fairly predictably from mid–May until the end of the second week in June.

Thereafter, fly hatches tend to fall off, and much of the trout's food during the 'dog days' of July and August is found amongst the weed, chiefly in the form of nymphs and freshwater shrimps. On overcast days, when the air is still or when there is a light south-westerly breeze, there may be hatches of iron blue duns or pale wateries during the day, and the fish may rise to them. And falls of spinners or hatches of sedges just before dusk may produce spectacular but often frustrating evening rises. But the bulk of the trout's feeding will be done below the surface.

It is not until September, when both the air and the water start to cool again, that hatches of upwinged flies will produce a flurry of surface feeding before the brown trout season closes at the end of the month or in October.

Some anglers regard what they call 'cannibal trout' with emotions ranging from contempt through awe to slight fear, apparently believing them to be almost a separate species from the brown trout they take on fly, or necessarily old and grizzly. In truth, though, all trout eat smaller fish than themselves from time to time, and a few become largely or exclusively piscivorous – usually because they have grown too big to be sustained by the insect and other invertebrate food forms available to them. Apart from this, these 'cannibals' are no different from any other brown trout.

EYESIGHT

A trout's eyes, set on either side of its head, have only a fairly narrow field of binocular vision but provide it with a very wide monocular arc, which enables it both to spot prey 'out of the corner of its eye' and to warn it of potential danger. The 'blind arc' behind a trout is quite narrow – no more than about 25° or 30°, but awareness of it can certainly make it easier for the angler to approach a fish unobserved.

There is no doubt that trout can identify colours in very much the same range as those that we see, but probably leaning towards the red end of the spectrum and possibly including one or two frequencies beyond the range of the human eye. If the flyfisher learns nothing else about the trout's senses, it is essential that he or she should at least develop a working understanding of the way in which fish see things in, on and above the water. All freshwater fish depend very heavily on their eyesight to warn them of impending danger, and most of them – particularly the predators – rely

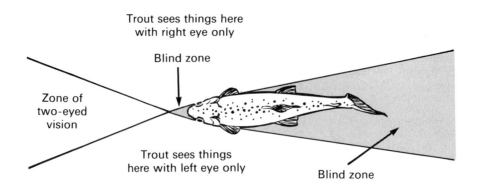

Trout sees things here
with right eye only

Blind zone

Zone of
two-eyed
vision

Trout sees things
here with left eye only

Blind zone

Blind arc — a bird's eye view of the trout's scene of vision

almost exclusively on it for the identification and taking of food items.
Because the ways in which light behaves in air and in water are very
different, the fish's visual perceptions of his surroundings are quite unlike
ours.

Three factors cause these differences – reflection from the water's surface,
refraction (the way in which light bends as it passes from air into water) and
colour absorption (the way in which various colours are progressively
filtered out as light passes down through the water). Colour absorption is of
greatest significance to the stillwater angler, who often works his fly or lure
at far greater depths than the stream or river flyfisher does, but reflection
and refraction are important to all of us.

Light striking the water's surface at 90° penetrates well and passes straight
down into it. As the angle of attack is reduced, so is the light's penetrating
power, more and more of it being reflected back off the water. The light
that does get through is refracted (bent) downwards. At an angle of attack
of about 20°, by far the greater part of the light is being reflected and the
small amount that does get through is being refracted downwards at an
angle of about 40°. At 10° and less, no light penetrates the surface at all.

The effect of all this is that a fish sees the underside of the water's surface
as a mirror in which are reflected the things around him and in the centre of
which, immediately above him, is a circular 'hole' or 'window', through
which he can see the outside world. Because the light's ability to penetrate
the surface decreases gradually as the angle of attack is reduced, rather than
simply stopping abruptly, the edge of the window is ill defined. And the

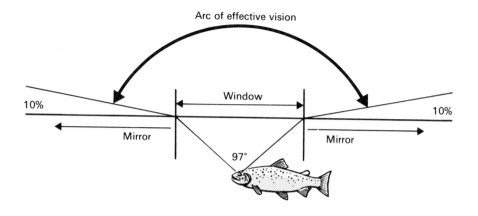

The fish's window

window for a fish lying deep in the water is larger than that for one lying close to the surface.

The immediate importance of this to the angler lies in the extent to which the fish can or cannot see him (and his rod) and the extent to which he may be able to use the blind area outside the fish's window to conceal himself. But there is far more to it than that.

In calm water, an unbroken mirror surrounding the fish's window affords a constant and, presumably, reassuring background to his life. Floating food forms borne down towards him on the current appear initially as indentations in the mirror. It is evident from their behaviour that trout learn to interpret these indentations. While it is still quite clearly beyond his window, a trout will start to lift in the water to intercept a natural fly, even apparently identifying a particular species on which he is feeding some time before he can see its body or wings. Thereafter, because of refraction, the fly's wings will appear in the trout's window, seemingly detached from the insect's body and 'suspended' in the air. Only when the fly's legs and feet appear in the window will the fish at last be able to see it as a complete entity. By this time, he has usually risen to meet it and is almost – but not quite – committed to taking it. From this it is evident that the initial impressions our flies make on the trout are important, and that his view of a fly is likely to be very different from our own – the 'feet' and wings being of primary significance.

The way in which a trout sees our fly line and leader is of considerable importance too. A floating fly line and a length of floating nylon both

23

appear in the mirror like great hawsers across the sky, and they look much bigger than they actually are because of the sizeable dent each makes in the surface film. If they are moved – when being retrieved, for example, or when being lifted off to be recast – they cause far more disturbance than may be evident from above the water. Obviously, all of this has serious implications in terms of our tackle's fish-frightening capabilities.

HEARING

The trout's next line of defence after his eyesight is his 'hearing'. Most fish do have vestigial or rudimentary ears, concealed beneath the skin at the backs of their skulls, roughly where ours are, but they seem to be relatively insensitive and I know of no evidence to suggest that they can pick up and interpret, for example, sounds beyond the water. Much more important to them are the vibration-sensitive cells located in their lateral lines – those convenient 'cut here' dotted lines that run down the centre of each side of the body from head to tail. These cells can detect the slightest resonance – footsteps on the bank or on a bridge or items being dropped or bumped in the bottom of a boat – and are used by trout almost exclusively as an alarm system.

TASTE AND SMELL

That trout have an adequately developed sense of taste and smell is of greater importance to the stillwater flyfisher than to those who fish streams or rivers, but is not vital to either. It seems probable that in lakes and reservoirs, where the fish often have time and opportunity to examine food items at leisure, some smells or flavours may attract them and they may find others repellent. Certainly they can sniff out sunken trout pellets in a stewpond, and there is some evidence that they find the smell of nicotine, for example, offensive. But in streams and rivers, where the food forms (and our artificial flies) are being swept along on the current and where the fish must decide fairly rapidly whether to take an approaching item or not, it seems clear that they rely almost exclusively on their eyesight for the identification and interception of their quarry.

THE SEA TROUT (*Salmo trutta*)

For many years, people believed brown trout and sea trout to be separate species, which is understandable because the two are so dramatically dissimilar in both appearance and habit. In fact, though, the sea trout is simply a migratory brown trout which, having been born and reared in a river, goes to sea when it is two or three years old and then spends the greater part of its adult life at sea, returning to the river of its birth only to spawn. It is during the sea trout's spawning run that the flyfisher goes in pursuit of it.

Although most of our chalk streams do have runs of sea trout, the spate rivers tend to have much better ones, and it is generally true that the less fertile a river is the better is its run of sea trout. This is probably because, over many hundreds of generations, brown trout in unfertile, relatively foodless waters have been under greater pressure to seek pastures new and some of them have therefore adopted a migratory habit.

The first time they return to fresh water from the sea, usually weighing between $\frac{1}{2}$ pound and 1 pound the sea trout tend to move in shoals, arriving between mid-June and late September. These first-run fish are known by an assortment of colloquial names – peal or school peal in Devon, herling and finnock in Scotland. Their older brothers and sisters, quite commonly weighing five or six pounds and sometimes very much more, arrive in the rivers in two runs – a generally light spring one, usually starting in April or May and going on into July, and an often heavier autumn one in September and October.

Sea trout can vary considerably in appearance. Some are virtually indistinguishable from non-migratory brown trout, having the same bronze or golden flanks and the same largish, lightly haloed black spots. Others – brilliantly silver and often with neat little black 'x' marks on their flanks – look more like salmon. They all present the flyfisher with an intriguing conundrum.

A fine bag of sea trout. Many flyfishers regard this migratory fish as the most challenging and rewarding of all British game species.

25

It is wholly provable and widely acknowledged that sea trout are indifferent to food in fresh water once they have been to sea, which is hardly surprising since so many of the rivers up which they run are so very barren. Rarely is anything found in their stomachs when they are caught. But they can be fished for and taken on exactly the same fly patterns we use for brown trout – specifically imitative ones, as well as the more commonly used traditional or attractor patterns. There can be few competent flyfishers who regularly go in pursuit of brown trout in streams and rivers in the West Country, in Wales or in Scotland who have not taken occasional sea trout on small dry flies.

The most significant characteristic of the sea trout from the angler's point of view – apart, perhaps, from its spectacular fight and its superb culinary qualities – is its shyness. Sea trout are infinitely more easily alarmed than brown trout are, and this militates in favour of fishing for them chiefly by night.

THE GRAYLING (*Thymallus thymallus*)

If the sea trout presents us with a conundrum, the grayling – the lady of the stream – is an enigma. Although quite unlike a trout in appearance and breeding habits, she wears the salmonid badge in the form of that small, tell-tale adipose fin on her back between dorsal fin and tail, and her diet is exactly the same as the trout's.

Grayling are rather more critical of water quality than brown trout are, and show a marked preference for cold, very clean, well oxygenated streams and rivers with plenty of deep, dark pools. Although they may be found in most parts of Great Britain, they do not occur in Ireland. On the mainland, they do best in the chalk streams and in spate rivers in Yorkshire, in the north country and in Scotland. (In north-west Europe – especially in Austria, Sweden, Finland and Norway – grayling fare noticeably better than they do here, and grow very much larger. In Britain, a two-pounder is a fine specimen and a three-pounder is exceptional.)

The grayling is a pretty and intriguing fish to look at. With her flat belly and gently arched back, she is beautifully streamlined – far more obviously so than the trout. Her markings – light grey or bronze on top blending to bright silver flanks lined laterally with black, and a white belly – are much like those of many coarse fish, as are her scales, which are noticeably larger than a trout's. But her single, most obvious distinguishing feature is her dorsal fin, huge, orange, barred and sail-like, which she uses to advantage when hooked – putting it up and 'paravaning' across the current – and which, apparently endearingly, but in fact for purely practical reasons, the male folds over his mate's back during spawning.

A grayling from the Hampshire Avon. The grayling is an enigma, bearing all the hallmarks of the salmonids and yet spawning with the coarse fish in the spring; but she extends the flyfisher's season into the autumn and winter.

The grayling's eye is interesting, too, with its strangely pear–shaped pupil which almost certainly serves to enhance her forward binocular vision.

The grayling is essentially a bottom feeder, as is evidenced by the fact that her mouth is on the small side and low–set, rather than being right at the front of her head as the trout's is. This probably accounts for the way in which she takes an insect from the water's surface, rising from the bottom increasingly steeply until she is almost lying on her back, and then turning sharply downwards having grabbed the fly – or, quite often, missed it. This is wholly different from the trout's gentle upward tilt from a position quite close to the surface, his confident taking of his quarry and his leisurely downward turn.

Unlike brown trout, grayling spawn in the spring with the coarse fish and, as a consequence, tend not to regain peak condition until the late summer, being at their best during the autumn and winter. They are prolific creatures, producing vast numbers of young which must be culled if any of them are to grow to respectable sizes and if they are not to encroach too heavily upon the trouts' food supplies. It is their prolific nature and the fact that their diets are so similar to the trout's that have brought about the contempt with which some anglers have regarded them and the wars that some keepers have waged on them.

But, if their numbers are kept within reasonable bounds, grayling are fine sporting fish and, in recent years, flyfishers have come to recognize this and to value the extension to the season they provide.

A chub. Growing to as much as 5 or 6 pounds in weight, chub may be taken on fly, but they are very shy.

A dace. The fast rising but diminutive dace can be used by the flyfisher to sharpen up his reactions in the late summer in preparation for the grayling season to come.

CHUB AND DACE (*Leuciscus cephalus* and *Leuciscus leuciscus*)

Neither chub nor dace are game fish in the accepted sense of that phrase but they are commonly encountered in trout waters, will take an artificial fly and can provide entertaining sport for flyfishers. They are widely distributed throughout England – although they are rare in the Lake District and are absent from Cornwall altogether – and they tend to inhabit the lower, slower-moving stretches of trout rivers, chiefly because they lay their eggs on fronds of weed, rather than in or on gravelly redds as trout and grayling

28

do, and weed is more plentiful in sedate waters than it is in fast-flowing ones.

In common with all other coarse fish, chub and dace spawn in late spring or early summer and do not fully recover condition until July or August. Although the young fish are very similar in appearance (they can be told apart by the convex trailing edge to the chub's anal fin as opposed to the dace's concave one), the adults are very different. Chub may grow to six pounds or more in weight and develop a distinctive bronzy hue; dace rarely reach a pound and remain bright silver.

As adults, the two species behave significantly differently, too. Chub tend to lurk beneath trees and overhanging bushes in small shoals of no more than a dozen or so, and they are intensely shy, sinking quietly to the bottom at the first sign of danger. Dace are far more open and gregarious, often lying in midstream in large shoals, and they seem to be markedly less easily frightened.

It is easy to dismiss chub and dace as vermin simply because they are inedible. But they are part of the flyfisher's heritage and are deserving of respect for the sport they may provide on hot and otherwise fishless afternoons, and for the service the dace can perform in honing the flyfisher's reactions in September in preparation for the grayling season to come.

THE RAINBOW TROUT (*Salmo gairdneri*)

Rainbow trout were first imported into Britain from their homes on the western seaboard of the United States during the 1880s. Since then, they have been increasingly widely farmed here, both for the table-fish market and for restocking purposes, and they have found their ways into a very substantial number of Britain's rivers, both by being stocked into them and by escaping from trout farms.

Although rainbow trout can, and do, breed successfully in far more of our rivers than is generally acknowledged, they are able to generate self-sustaining populations in only very few. It is one thing for rainbows to deposit ova in the redds and for some of the ova to hatch; it is quite another for the juvenile fish to survive and reach maturity in substantial numbers and, themselves, to breed successfully. The only British rivers which now appear to support significant, self-regenerating populations of rainbow trout are the Dove and the Wye in Derbyshire, the Missbourne on the Hertfordshire–Buckinghamshire border, the Buckinghamshire Wye (where they breed in the feeder streams which run into the lake at West Wycombe Park and then thrive in the lake), and possibly one or two small Hampshire chalk brooks. There used to be a reasonable head of naturalized

The rainbow trout is an alien species which breeds in few British rivers but which has been stocked into some and escaped into many more from fish farms.

rainbow trout in the River Chess in Hertfordshire, but post-war abstraction and pollution seem to have destroyed it.

Young rainbow trout, bright silver in colour, can readily be distinguished from salmon and sea trout smolts and from juvenile brown trout by the dark spots which extend onto their tails and by the relative roundness of the tails themselves. As adults, they are clearly identifiable by the broad, iridescent, pinkish band which runs down their flanks from head to tail and, again, by the fact that they are the only salmonid species to have spots on their tails.

Fast-growing, disease-resistant, tolerant of being crowded together in stewponds and with a markedly higher temperature tolerance range than the brown's, rainbow trout are ideal farm fish and can provide excellent sport in lakes and reservoirs. However, like many others, I have grave doubts as to whether they should ever be stocked into streams or rivers. They are voracious feeders (which accounts for their rapid growth) and are inclined to shoal, especially when immature; they therefore compete very heavily with brown trout for food and will frequently harass the more sedate browns quite unmercifully.

Rainbow trout also tend to have a strong migratory urge, often heading off downstream almost as soon as they are put into the water. When they do settle down in an area, they seem to be listless, roaming much further in search of food than brown trout do. One of the chief pleasures of river flyfishing is the stalking of individual fish, and there can be few things more frustrating than to spend five or ten minutes on hands and knees, working your way into a position from which you can cast to a particular trout, only to find when you get there that it has wandered off to pastures new.

Finally, my own experience suggests that rainbow trout rarely do as well in rivers as they might be expected to. I have no idea why this should be – any more than I understand why they so rarely breed successfully in Britain – but I have caught far more than just occasional sad, dull, lank and flaccid specimens from streams and rivers, and the only really bright, deep, fit ones I have found have been those that have taken up residence immediately downstream from stewponds where they have been able to feed on surplus pellets washed down to them on the current.

EELS (*Anguilla anguilaa*) – Just for Fun

I am assured by that most excellent flyfisher Brian Clarke, and the story is confirmed by Fred Buller, one of the country's greatest experts on freshwater fish, that there are carriers and side-streams on the River Test on which falls of spinners can be so heavy at certain times of year that the resident eels have been seen there, lying just beneath the surface and rising to the spent flies just as trout do.

I am not aware that anyone has ever taken an eel on a dry fly (although I know they are quite often caught on deep-sunk lures on stillwaters), but it might be fun to try!

3

THE

TROUT'S FOOD

As we saw in the previous chapter, trout in streams and rivers have remarkably catholic diets, feeding on a vast array of aquatic and terrestrial insects and other invertebrates as well as occasionally on small fish. In this chapter I shall consider the characteristics and life-cycles of the main orders of aquatic insects upon which trout and grayling live in running water, a couple of other basic aquatic food forms and, relatively briefly, the main terrestrial creatures they take advantage of when the opportunity presents itself. A series of detailed regional charts, giving identifying particulars of specific species, their seasons and some of the artificials with which they may be represented, is provided at Appendix I.

Essentially, the aquatic insects that form the staple diets of trout in streams and rivers can be divided into four main groups – upwinged flies, sedge flies, stoneflies and flat-winged flies. A basic understanding of the distribution, appearance and life-cycle of each of these groups is important to the angler as it can help him to identify what the fish are feeding on and to select an appropriate artificial from his fly box. The descriptions that follow cover the main insect families: detailed descriptions of the individual species may be found in the tables on pages 145–153.

THE UPWINGED FLIES (*Ephemeroptera*)

Upwinged flies are found, in greater or lesser numbers, on every stream and river in Great Britain. In their various forms they constitute a substantial part of the trout's food intake and, perhaps with the sedge flies, they are the cornerstone upon which river flyfishing – and especially dry-fly fishing – is based.

Some twenty species of upwinged flies are of consequence to fish, and therefore to fishermen – from the tiny caenis at less than $\frac{1}{4}$ inch long to the mayfly, which averages $\frac{3}{4}$ inch in length, excluding its tails. Their life-cycles are all similar, and begin when eggs are laid on the water's surface or, in some species, beneath it.

The nymphs that hatch from the eggs vary in appearance and habit. Some are relatively flat, which enables them to cling to stones in fast running water. Others are well camouflaged and slow-moving bottom dwellers. Many are slim and streamlined and can swim rapidly from weed frond to weed frond. One, the mayfly nymph, is strong and bullet-headed, which enables it to burrow into mud and silt on the river bed.

For all their differences, the nymphs of all upwinged flies have many visible characteristics in common. Each has six legs, a small head, a relatively bulbous thorax, which becomes darker and increasingly hump-backed as the nymph matures and the wings develop beneath it, a segmented abdomen with gill filaments along either side, and three tails.

As they develop, the nymphs feed busily on decaying vegetable matter – rotting weed, fallen leaves, and so on. A year after the egg from which it was hatched was laid, each nymph prepares to rise to the water's surface and hatch as an adult fly. This is a fascinating process. Most species build up a gaseous layer between their bodies and their outer casings, which probably serves both to increase their buoyancy, helping them in their ascent through the water, and to separate the now fully formed adult fly from its nymphal shuck.

When conditions are right, the nymph part-swims and part-floats to the surface, where it pushes through the surface film while the nymphal case splits along the back and the adult fly, the dun, emerges. This can be an astonishingly rapid process, sometimes almost instantaneous.

The duns of all the upwinged species are dull, drab, lustreless creatures, with opaque wings and short, often rather limp-looking tails. They remain on the surface of the river only for as long as it takes for their wings to stiffen and dry, being easy pickings for trout while they do so. An upwinged dun's body and legs are not greatly dissimilar to those of the nymph, although the head may be a little larger and the legs are markedly longer. Some species have two large wings, others have a further pair of much smaller ones located behind (usually overlapping) their main ones.

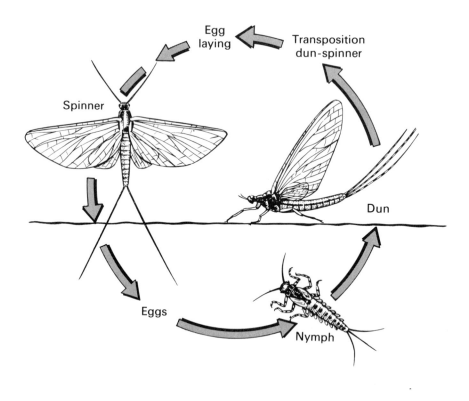

The life cycle of an upwinged fly

As soon as they are able to, the duns fly up from the water and into trees, bushes or other bankside vegetation, where they remain for anything from twelve to thirty-six hours before 'rehatching'. This is one of the most intriguing and miraculous transformations in nature. Clinging to a leaf or twig, the dun parts its wings and its back splits open, just as the nymph's did, and another fully developed fly, the spinner, emerges complete and perfect in every detail. The spinner is a markedly brighter, prettier creature than the dun, with a shiny body, glistening, transparent wings, longer forelegs and either two or three slender tails depending on species, each as much as twice or three times the insect's body length.

Upwinged spinners usually mate in flight, often repeatedly dancing upwards and drifting down again in the air above the river and the river bank as they do so – a lovely sight against the setting sun on a summer evening. The males die almost as soon as mating has been completed. The females then lay their eggs on the water, dipping onto it repeatedly in the process, before dying themselves, floating away spreadeagled on the current. In a few species, the female crawls down a reed stem or the woodwork of a groyne or footbridge to lay her eggs actually in the water.

Trout feed on the nymphs of upwinged flies wherever and whenever they can find them, on the duns waiting on the surface for their wings to dry, and on the spinners, especially as they lie inert on top of the water.

THE SEDGE FLIES (*Trichoptera*)

Of the almost two hundred species of sedge flies identified in Britain, only about twenty are of any consequence to flyfishers and fewer still are of interest on streams and rivers. Nevertheless, those few are of considerable importance.

The female sedges lay their eggs on the water's surface or by crawling beneath it, very much as the upwinged flies do, and the eggs sink to the river bed or adhere to weed, where they eventually hatch as larvae. Sedge larvae (often called caddis grubs) vary from $\frac{1}{4}$ inch to 1 inch in length. Ponderous and juicy, they are extremely vulnerable to predation by trout and other fish and seek to protect themselves by building cases around their bodies, which are rather like legless caterpillars. They construct the cases from a wide variety of bits and pieces – mud, grains of sand, discarded tiny snail shells, bits of twig and reed stem cut to length. Each species is particular about the material it uses and the method of construction, and the case serves both to camouflage the larva and – to some extent – to protect it physically from predators. With their bodies safely encased and just their heads and legs sticking out, the larvae lumber about the river bed feeding on decaying vegetation and, occasionally, other smaller insects.

At its appointed time the larva retreats into its case, eventually to emerge as a pupa. The pupal phase in the insect's life is a relatively brief and transitory one, serving only as the stage of transition from the river bed to the water's surface, where the adult fly hatches. The pupae of some sedge species climb clear of the water to hatch, while others simply hatch in the surface film, where their desperate, scuttling efforts to get airborne make them attractive targets for trout.

At rest, adult sedges are not unlike moths in general appearance, folding their four wings into neat roof shapes over their backs. But their wings are, in fact, covered with very fine hairs, while a moth's are scaled, and they

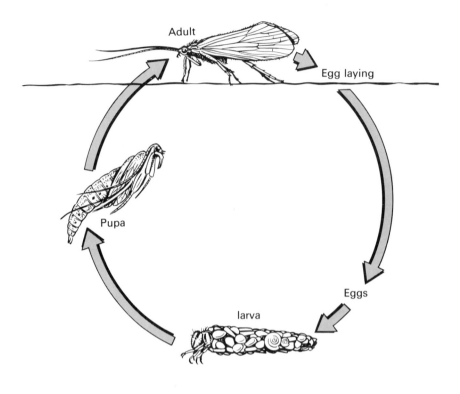

The life cycle of the sedge fly

generally have distinctively long antennae. Adult sedges mate on shore and amongst the waterside vegetation, rather than in flight, the females returning to the water to lay their eggs and, again, to become vulnerable to predation by fish.

Although trout eat sedge larvae and pupae, river flyfishers generally concentrate their attentions on the winged adults for both practical and traditional reasons. The practical basis for this is the difficulty of fishing an artificial sedge larva realistically slowly on the river or stream bed where the naturals live. The traditional one probably has to do with reservations about fishing necessarily heavily weighted 'nymphs' to trout in streams and rivers. (This is, of course, entirely at variance with stillwater flyfishing practice, where artificial sedge larva and pupa patterns are standard weapons in the angler's armoury.)

THE STONEFLIES (*Plecoptera*)

The stoneflies, of which there are some thirty species in Britain are found in and on the banks of stony rivers, chiefly in Scotland, Ireland and the north of England. Where they occur elsewhere, they generally do so in numbers too small to be of any real interest to fish or fishermen. The exception, perhaps, is the willow fly which may be seen on and around gravel-bedded rivers throughout the United Kingdom in August and September.

Stoneflies have only three-phase life-cycles. The nymphs hatch from eggs stuck to stones and rocks on the river bed and live on the bottom, moulting as many as thirty times before eventually clambering ashore to hatch. They are strong crawlers and are readily identifiable from the nymphs of upwinged flies by the fact that they have only two, quite short, jointed tails and by their two relatively long antennae. They range from $\frac{1}{4}$ inch to just over 1 inch in length and, while the smaller species feed on algae and organic debris, the larger ones are fearsome predators, preying on caddis and fly larvae and even on the nymphs of other stoneflies.

The nymphal (or creeper) stage of the stonefly's life lasts for between one and three years, depending upon the species. At the end of this time, it crawls ashore for its final moult, which produces the winged adult.

Like the nymphs, the adults each have two antennae and two tails. Their wings, set in two pairs, are hard and glossy, and are laid curved over their backs in a somewhat shell-like configuration when the insects are at rest.

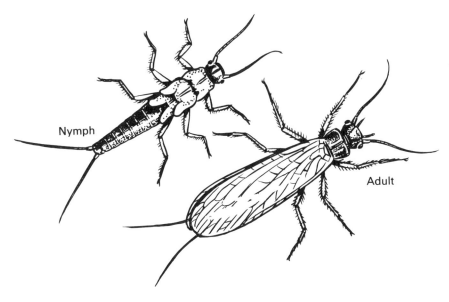

Nymph

Adult

The Stone fly

The female is generally the better flyer (if still a little clumsy) and, in some species, the male's wings are almost vestigial, covering no more than half the length of the insect's body and being effectively useless.

Adult stoneflies are essentially land-based creatures. They scuttle around amongst the rocks and boulders on the river bank, rarely moving far from the water, and they mate on land. Having done so, the female flies back to the water where she deposits her eggs – some species walk across the surface depositing small clumps of ova as they go, others dip repeatedly onto the water, and one or two simply 'crash land', releasing all their eggs at once as they do so.

Trout and particularly grayling feed on stonefly nymphs, nosing around amongst the pebbles on the bottom in search of them, and they also take the egg-laying females enthusiastically.

THE FLAT-WINGED FLIES (Diptera)

The order *Diptera* is one of the largest in the insect world, including all the houseflies, midges, mosquitoes, daddy-long-legs, and so on. Surprisingly few of its members are of interest to fish or flyfishers and, of those that are, the majority are of far greater importance on still waters than on streams and rivers. However, midges have largely been ignored by river anglers (if not by trout), quite possibly to our cost.

Midges have four-stage life-cycles. Female midges lay their eggs in gelatinous clumps either on the water's surface or on weed fronds. The larvae that eventually hatch vary enormously in size ($\frac{1}{8}$ inch to over 1 inch) and colour (from grey through assorted shades of green and brown to red), but are all slender and worm-like in appearance and propel themselves with a peculiar, figure-of-eight lashing movement. Having hatched, they sink to the river bed, where they live among the decaying vegetation upon which they feed.

At their appointed times, the larvae pupate, the emergent pupae being distinctively comma-shaped. Each one has a somewhat bulbous thorax, from which protrudes a tuft of breathing filaments, and a slender, curved, usually clearly segmented abdomen tipped with a tiny bunch of gill fibres. When they are ready to hatch, the pupae, quite competent swimmers, make their way to the top of the water. There they lie horizontally suspended under the surface film before splitting to release the adult midge. This hatching process is usually very quick, the winged adults flying off at once, rather than spending any time on the surface.

Adult midges mate in flight, often forming tall, smoky columns in the lee of trees, hedgerows and buildings on warm evenings, the females then returning to the water to lay their eggs.

Trout feed keenly on midge larvae and pupae. The emergent adult flies generally get airborne too quickly after hatching to present easy pickings, but trout do take females trapped, dead or dying in the surface film after egg laying.

Midge larvae – tiny, slow-moving and bottom-dwelling – are virtually impossible for the river flyfisher to represent with an artificial (although the wobble-worm, which I devised for use on stillwaters, can be effective). I am convinced, however, that there is room for a great deal more experimentation than has yet been done with small midge pupa patterns – probably in sizes 12 to 16 – fished as nymphs just beneath the surface film, and with 'damp' imitations of the spent adult.

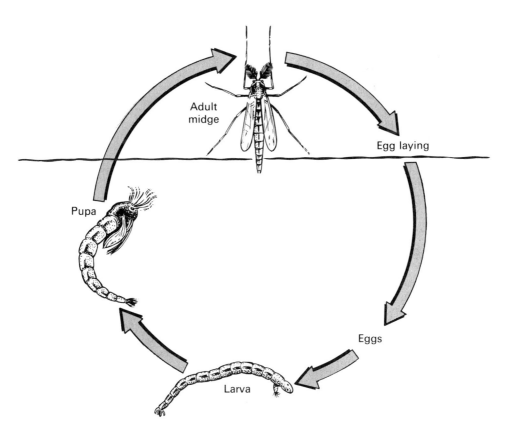

The life cycle of the midge

MISCELLANEA

THE ALDER (*Sialis lutaria*)

Although ¾-inch long, dark-brown, seemingly sedge-like alderflies appear in large numbers throughout Britain in May, and although artificials, both wet and dry, dressed to represent them can be very effective, I know of no evidence to suggest that trout actually feed on the naturals. I do not therefore propose to describe the fly's life-cycle or behaviour in any detail, but instead simply recommend the artificials as useful general patterns.

THE FRESHWATER SHRIMP (*Gammarus pulex*)

Freshwater shrimps are found in all clean, alkaline streams and rivers in Britain, often in prodigious numbers. Averaging about ½ inch in length, they curl themselves up when at rest and straighten out as they start to swim. Seeking shelter in the weed and amongst the pebbles on the stream bed, they are a dull, light yellow-ochre colour for most of the year, turning a much deeper orange-yellow as the mating season approaches in spring or early summer.

Trout and grayling feed on shrimps enthusiastically, foraging around amongst the weed roots for them, sometimes, in shallow streams, with their tails waving in the air in a rather silly way. The fish may be taken on any of the several artificials designed to represent the shrimp or on Frank Sawyer's Killer Bug, a patently shrimp-like pattern.

Heavily weighted shrimp patterns can be useful for winkling trout out of unusually deep, difficult lies. Speaking purely personally, though, and while

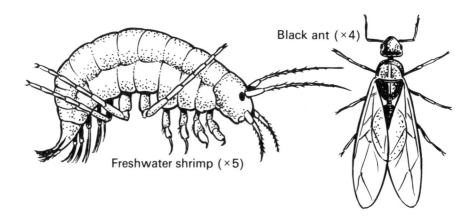

Black ant (×4)

Freshwater shrimp (×5)

All kinds of insect are eaten by trout – see also page 42

I have no reservations whatever about using leaded dressings on stillwaters, I am inclined to reserve them on rivers for otherwise wholly inaccessible fish, rather than to resort to them as regular panaceas when there are almost always more delicate and subtle options available.

TERRESTRIAL INSECTS

Trout and, to a lesser extent, grayling are opportunistic feeders, cheerfully accepting almost any living food form that presents itself to them. The following list of the main terrestrial food forms, with descriptions of their appearances, seasons and suggested artificials, will enable the reader to anticipate the most important of the myriad land-born species and to make the most of them as and when they occur.

ANTS (*Hymenoptera*)

Sure-footed as they are, ants rarely fall onto the water from bankside vegetation or overhanging branches, and are therefore surprisingly rarely available to trout in the normal course of events. But, from time to time, usually on heavy, humid, thundery days in mid- to late summer, they develop wings and take to the air. When this happens, they are sometimes blown onto the water in great numbers, and the fish take full advantage of this manna from heaven. Flights of ants always seem to last for less than a week, and falls of them on streams and rivers rarely continue for more than a couple of hours or so, but the angler with a few appropriate artificials in his fly box can have a field day during that time.

BEETLES (*Coleoptera*)

Unlike ants, all shapes, sizes and colours of beetles come to grief on the water, and they appear at all stages of the season. They can make a significant contribution to the diets of trout in small, heather-girt and otherwise relatively barren upland streams and in streams and rivers heavily overhung with trees and bushes.

Although some species – most notably the soldier and sailor beetles and the Coch-y-bondu – are well known to anglers, being blown onto the water in large numbers (usually in mid-summer), there are in fact so many different species that may become available to the trout that it is probably best simply to rely on one or two general patterns with which to represent them all. The artificial Coch-y-bondu is reasonably reliable for this purpose, as is its close relative the Black and Peacock Spider. While some modern artificials have been devised specifically to imitate particular beetles, my own experience suggests that they appeal more to fishermen than fish, the latter preferring more general dressings.

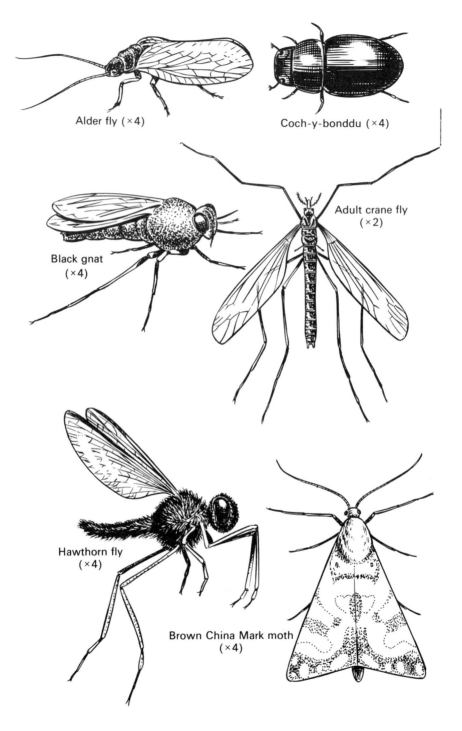

Alder fly (×4)

Coch-y-bonddu (×4)

Black gnat (×4)

Adult crane fly (×2)

Hawthorn fly (×4)

Brown China Mark moth (×4)

Terrestrial insects forming the trout's diet (scale in brackets)

BLACK GNATS AND REED SMUTS (*Bibio* spp and *Simulium* spp)
Black gnat is a generic term used by flyfishers to encompass several small
($\frac{1}{4}$-inch long), black flat-winged terrestrial fly species which may be blown
onto streams and rivers at almost any stage in the season, from May until
September. Black gnats are always warmly welcomed by trout and, as falls
of them are so common, they are of considerable importance to flyfishers.
They seem to be most vulnerable to the wind when mating, so the widely
available Knotted Black Gnat artificial, which has hackles at the front and
back of its body, is usually highly effective.

Reed smuts are similar to black gnats in appearance, but very much
smaller. While the trout feed on them greedily, and can sometimes become
preoccupied with them, they are really too small to be imitated or
represented on a hook.

THE CRANEFLIES (*Tipula* spp)
The cranefly or daddy-long-legs is another terrestrial flat-winged fly which
is quite often blown onto the water, especially in grassland areas, to the
benefit of the trout and, occasionally, the angler. Craneflies are much in
evidence during the late summer, from the end of August onwards, and are
instantly recognizable by their extraordinarily long gangling legs and their
quite remarkable lack of control in the air. Because they are wholly wind-
borne, they are probably of more interest to trout on large lakes and
reservoirs than they are on streams and rivers. On stillwaters, they can be
blown onto the water in sufficient numbers for the fish to become
accustomed to them and to accept them as a regular part of their diets. On
running water, and particularly on narrow streams, I suspect that they reach
the water too occasionally to be of any real consquence to the fish.
Nevertheless, where a river runs through meadowland, the flyfisher with
an artificial daddy or two in his box at the back end of the summer may
well have an advantage over the one who has not.

THE HAWTHORN FLY (*Bibio marci*)
The hawthorn fly is one of nature's great gifts to trout and to trout fishers
early in the season. From $\frac{1}{2}$ inch to $\frac{3}{4}$ inch long, with a furry jet-black body,
translucent grey wings and two extraordinarily distinctive long, trailing
black legs, it appears towards the end of April, remains with us until about
mid-May and is often blown onto the water in considerable numbers.
When it is, the fish take it unhesitatingly and seem to be almost as uncritical
of an artificial as they are of the natural.

It is said that the natural sinks when it arrives on the water. Although I
have had many excellent days fishing during falls of hawthorn flies, I have
not been able fully to confirm this, but it is certainly true that a 'damp'

43

pattern, fished in or just below the surface film, often seems to be more effective than a high-floating dry one.

MOTHS (*Lepidoptera*)
Although they only fall or are blown onto the water individually and occasionally, moths are often taken greedily by trout, possibly because of their size and evident helplessness, and an artificial can sometimes deceive even the most difficult fish, particularly late in the evening.

Choice of pattern does not seem to be too critical – almost any cream or brown one may be tied on with reasonable confidence. Personally, I have had some considerable success – and my biggest ever brown trout from a river – with a bushy white pattern tied with a soft, floppy cree hackle.

4

THE TACKLE

FOR THE JOB

Unlike coarse anglers and, to a lesser extent, those who go in pursuit of trout in lakes and reservoirs, stream and river flyfishers are wanderers, and must go lightly laden. Neil Patterson, one of the best flyfishers I know, carries nothing but a rod, a few flies stuck into a sheepskin patch pinned to his shirt and a spare spool of tippet nylon in his pocket. Few of us would choose to fish as sparsely equipped as that, but the example is a valuable one. Wear a fishing waistcoat if you will (I do) – it will enable you to carry everything you need neatly stored and ready to hand – but creels, fishing bags, picnic baskets, fish basses and suitcases full of flies have no place at the riverside.

Which is not to say that we should not take with us what we need or that we can get away with ill chosen or ill matched tackle. Good, well balanced equipment is essential both to confidence and to consistent success (the two go hand in hand), and two of the great benefits of river flyfishing are that we need relatively little tackle and that even the very best is not outrageously expensive.

It might seem logical to choose a rod first and then to match the fly line or lines to it. In fact, it is not. The weight and profile of the line to be used is dictated by the size and nature of the water we mean to fish, and the line

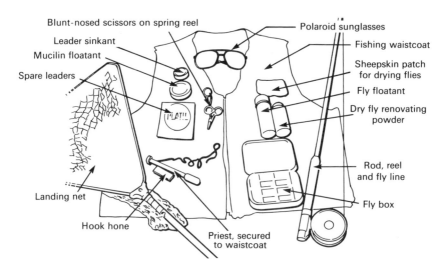

Blunt-nosed scissors on spring reel
Leader sinkant
Mucilin floatant
Spare leaders

Polaroid sunglasses
Fishing waistcoat
Sheepskin patch
for drying flies
Fly floatant
Dry fly renovating
powder

Landing net

Rod, reel
and fly line

Fly box

Hook hone

Priest, secured
to waistcoat

The stream and river flyfisher's tackle.

should therefore be chosen first, a suitable rod subsequently being matched to it.

FLY LINES

Fly lines, generally consisting of a braided dacron core covered with a plastic coating, provide the weight that is used to 'work' the fly rod when casting and to roll the line out over the water, presenting the fly (we hope) delicately and accurately. They come in a bewildering array of profiles, weights, densities and colours. The first three of these factors are reduced to an Association of Fishing Tackle Manufacturers' (AFTM) code, printed on the box (for example DT5F); the fourth is self-evident.

The first letter or letters of the code indicate whether a line is level (L), double-tapered (DT), weight-forward (WF) or a shooting head or shooting taper (ST). The number represents the weight in drams of the first ten yards of the line, excluding the two feet of level line at the end. And the last letter or letters show whether the line is a floater (F), a sinker (S), a sink-tip (F/S) or an intermediate (I). So our DT5F is a double-tapered floating line, the first ten yards of which weigh five drams. Similarly, a WF7F/S would be a weight-forward line, the first ten yards weighing seven drams, the front ten yards sinking and the remainder floating.

Level lines are exactly what their name implies, having the same diameter throughout their lengths. While they are relatively cheap, they are rather difficult to cast with and offer no practical advantage over any of the other profiles. Very few flyfishers use them, and they are now almost unobtainable.

A double-tapered line is level for two feet at each end, then tapers over ten feet to a markedly heavier centre section twenty-two yards long. It is relatively easy to cast with, turns over neatly, can be made to land lightly on the water and has the added advantage of being reversible. That is to say, when one end becomes worn the line can be reversed on the reel, extending its life probably by a further full season or two. (The reversibility of a double-tapered line does not double its life as some manufacturers would have you believe. From the moment it is taken from its wrapping, a fly line starts to dry out, the plasticizer which provides its suppleness evaporating. By the time it has been in use for two or three seasons, the back half will have lost almost as much plasticizer as the front half and will be becoming prone to wear and cracking. The tubs of replasticizer available from some tackle shops will rejuvenate a line temporarily but can only extend its life for a season or so.)

Weight-forward lines are level for their first two feet, then taper up over ten feet to a substantially heavier ten-yard belly, tapering down again quite

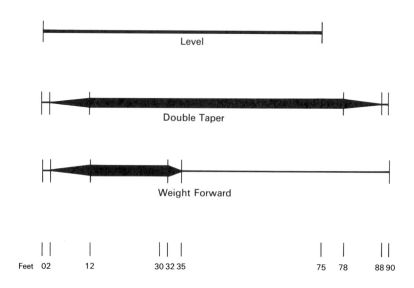

Level

Double Taper

Weight Forward

Feet 02   12   30 32 35   75   78   88 90

Typical fly line profiles

steeply to some eighteen yards of fine, level, running line. They are a little less easy to cast with than double-tapers (and rapidly go out of control if the belly is extended beyond the rod tip during casting), and they tend to land on the water rather less delicately than a double-taper does. But they do enable the angler to cast further than he could with a double-taper. Weight-forward lines are chiefly of use on stillwaters, where distance casting is often called for, but there may be a place for one in the armoury of the flyfisher who regularly fishes large rivers.

In profile, a shooting head is essentially the front third to a half of a double-tapered line spliced at its thickest point to a fine running line – usually of braided nylon or flattened nylon monofilament. Although some stillwater anglers can cast prodigious distances with shooting heads, the backing line always seems to be prone to tangling and to be uncomfortable to handle, and there is little to be said for the use of shooting heads on streams or rivers.

Long-belly lines are essentially weight-forwards with their weight spread over a greater length. They are said to combine some of the distance casting capability of a weight-forward with some of the delicacy of a double-taper. They are primarily of use to those who fish large lakes or reservoirs.

The mathematics involved in the calculation of line weights are of little consequence to the practical angler, but it is important to understand which weights are best suited to which purposes.

Lines rated #3 and below are generally considered too light and susceptible to the wind to be of any real use at all except, perhaps, to the most enthusiastic light-line aficionados. Lines rated #8 and over are too heavy and indelicate for trout fishing on streams and rivers. So, for most of our purposes, we should consider lines in the range #4 to #7. In fact, #4s, still on the light side, are probably best reserved for small streams and brooks, and for very clear chalk streams, where accuracy and delicacy are at a premium and where distance casting is almost never required. And somewhat heavy #7s are usually used only on large rivers where it may be necessary to put out a long line occasionally. So we are chiefly interested in lines rated #5 or #6.

Floating lines are by far the most widely used for flyfishing on streams and rivers. Rarely is the water deep enough to justify the use of a sinking line or a sink-tip. A floating line can be lifted from the water and recast quickly, whereas a sinker or sink-tip must either be retrieved and recast or the angler must do a roll cast to bring the line to the surface before recasting. And floating lines are far less likely to snag on weed beds and other underwater obstructions than sinkers or sink-tips are in running water.

Nevertheless, even though they are less easy to cast with than floating lines (because they are made up from two lines of different densities), there may be a place for a sink-tip on a large river, especially when fishing for sea trout or grayling lying well down in deep pools. And it can be argued that an intermediate (which has almost neutral buoyancy) or a slow sinker may be useful for the same purpose or when fishing a nymph for trout or grayling on a deep and reasonably weed-free river. It is certainly true that sinking lines create far less surface disturbance than floating ones do and that they are, therefore, far less obvious to the fish.

Fly line colour is a subject to which the manufacturers have paid far too little attention. Although there are a few exceptions nowadays, floating lines are generally made in light hues – pale blue, ivory, peach and even white – and sinking ones are made in darker ones, usually browns or greens. In fact, there is incontrovertible evidence to show that the flash from a light coloured line in the air and the gleaming white streak it makes across the mirror beyond the fish's window are both startlingly evident from the trout's viewpoint and must be one of the commonest causes of alarm in our quarry. Those who doubt this should study the remarkable photographs in Brian Clarke and John Goddard's most excellent book, *The Trout and the Fly*. It is possible (and sensible) to dye your own fly lines, but the sooner a manufacturer starts producing a good-quality, mid- to dark grey or brown, matt-surfaced floating line the better.

As for quality, there is no doubt that where fly lines are concerned you get what you pay for. So always buy the best line or lines you can afford.

FLY RODS

MATERIALS

The materials most widely used for making fly rods today are cane, fibreglass and carbon fibre. Each has its advantages and disadvantages; good, bad and indifferent rods are available in all three materials.

Cane rods are built from carefully cut and bonded triangular sections of male Tonkin bamboo. They still have a large following, especially among experienced and traditionally minded river flyfishers. Length for length they are heavier than their fibreglass and carbon–fibre counterparts, but they often have gentle actions and can deliver a fly accurately and delicately. They are expensive, though, and, sentiment apart, offer little real advantage over fibreglass or carbon fibre.

Fibreglass rods are less expensive than either cane or carbon-fibre ones, but tend to be rather soft-actioned and have now largely been superseded by carbon fibre.

When carbon fibre was introduced for rod making a dozen or so years ago, it was claimed to have almost magical properties, particularly in terms of casting distance. In fact, some of the early carbon-fibre rods were abominable creations (just as some of the early fibreglass ones had been).

Three old friends. The author's favourite stream and river fly rods. Left to right: a 7-foot cane rod for fishing small, overgrown streams; an 8-foot 6-inch fibreglass one used on everything from small brooks to quite large rivers; and a 10-foot carbon fibre rod for sea trout fishing on large rivers.

LARGE STONE FLY

LAST HOPE

LUNN'S PARTICULAR

MARCH BROWN

PALMERED SEDGE

PHEASANT TAIL

ROUGH OLIVE

SHERRY SPINNER

WHITE MOTH

WICKMAN'S FANCY

YELLOW SALLY

YELLOW TAG

PHEASANT TAIL NYMPH

GREY GOOSE NYMPH

OLIVE NYMPH

GHRE NYMPH

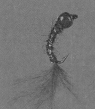

WOBBLE WORM

MIDGE PUPA

KILLER BUG

SHRIMP

LARGE STONEFLY
NYMPH

ADULT MIDGE

ALDER

BLACK AND
PEACOCK SPIDER

COCH-Y-BONDU

BLUE UPRIGHT

BLUE UPRIGHT SPIDER

GREENWELL'S
SPIDER

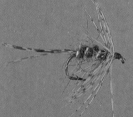

MARCH BROWN SPIDER

PARTRIDGE AND
ORANGE

POULT BLOA

SNIPE AND
PURPLE

WATERHEN
BLOA

RED TAG

YELLOW SALLY

WILLIAMS FAVOURITE

However, the initial teething troubles have now largely been resolved and, although still more expensive than fibreglass, carbon fibre has now come down quite dramatically in price. Today, carbon-fibre rods sales constitute by far the greater part of the rod market.

Carbon fibre has three major qualities. It is light – which makes for effortless casting over long periods. It is strong – rods made from it are therefore slender and cut through the wind efficiently. And the tip of a carbon rod stops dead at the end of a forward cast instead of bouncing up and down, enabling the skilful angler to put out a straighter line than he might otherwise be able to.

Two warnings should be issued in relation to carbon-fibre rods.

First, 'carbon fibre' is, in fact, made by marrying fibreglass and carbon fibres. In order to produce cheap rods, the manufacturers of some blanks have reduced the actual carbon content significantly but continued to make very light and slender rods with the debased material. The resultant rods tend to be both limper in action and markedly more fractile than those with a higher carbon content. It is almost always a false economy to buy a very cheap 'carbon-fibre' rod.

Second, carbon-fibre rods (of any quality) are relatively fragile. Working them with insufficient line extended can set up stresses leading to instantaneous breakage, usually six or eight inches above the handle, and a nick caused by a fly striking the rod during casting can cause similar weakness, the fracture often occurring without warning weeks or months later.

Regardless of what a rod is made of, three other factors should influence our choice – line rating, length and action.

LINE RATING

Nowadays, every good fly rod is marked just above the handle with the weight of line or the range of line weights to which it is best suited, for example #5 or #4–6 (an experienced tackle dealer should be able to advise you if you have an old, unmarked rod). This rating assumes that ten yards of line will be aerialized. For every two yards more or less aerialized in actual fishing, the line needs to be one size lighter or heavier to load the rod correctly. So if you usually fish a small brook on which you rarely expect to cast further than about eight yards, you should 'overload' your rod by one number – for example, by using a #5 line on a #4 rod.

Beware of rods rated for a wide range of line weights. Whatever a manufacturer may claim, every rod must have a line weight to which it is best suited, and to move away from this optimum must inevitably inhibit the rod's performance. Personally, I am very wary of any rod marked with anything more than two, adjacent, AFTM numbers – for example, #4–5.

LENGTH

Perhaps slightly surprisingly, the lengths of rods used for stream and river fishing vary more than do those of rods used on stillwaters. For most purposes, on the chalk streams and on medium-sized spate rivers, an 8½-foot or a 9-foot rod will serve very well. But on small becks and brooks, heavily overhung with trees and bushes, it may be necessary to go down to 7½ or even 7 feet in order to be able to work a line out without constantly catching leaves and branches. And on large rivers, a 10-foot rod may barely be long enough to cover the water and to keep in touch with one's flies, especially when fishing a wet fly or a team of wet flies upstream.

On the whole, it is sensible to buy a slightly longer rod than you think you need, rather than a shorter one. Although 7-foot and 7½-foot wands are very pretty, they can pose quite serious problems when fishing from the bank; they make it difficult to cast and to retrieve line over reeds, rushes and nettles, to control the line on the water, and to play fish, especially in heavily weeded waters. Unless you habitually wade beneath a canopy of foliage, an 8½-foot or even a 9-foot rod should not prove too long for even the smallest stream, and it should be long enough to cope with all but the largest rivers.

ACTION

Any fly rod's action is described in terms of the part of its length over which it bends most freely and of its overall stiffness or flexibility.

A rod which is stiff throughout most of its length and only starts to flex easily towards its tip is said to be 'tip-actioned'; one that bends near its butt is said to be 'butt-actioned'; and one that flexes progressively from butt to tip is said to have an 'all-through' action. Regardless of whereabouts a rod flexes along its length, the amount that it will bend under a given load is described in terms of stiffness or softness.

A tip-actioned rod demands a fairly brisk casting action and the loop of the line as it turns over at the ends of the forward and back casts tends to be fairly narrow, which makes for good casting into a wind. The nearer the action gets to the butt, the slower the casting action and the wider the loop. A slow- or butt-actioned rod will present a fly more delicately than a fast- or tip-actioned one, but will be less effective in cutting through a breeze. Most river flyfishers find that a moderately stiff all-through action will meet most of their needs.

A two-piece rod should always be preferred to a three-piece one except where shortness is essential for portability. However well they are made, joints interfere with a rod's action, so the fewer the better. Modern spigot ferrules have less effect on rod action than do the more traditional metal ones.

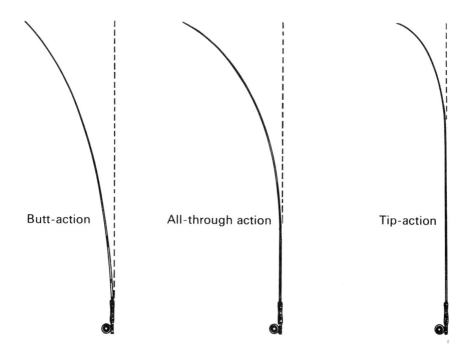

Butt-action   All-through action   Tip-action

Typical rod actions

A brief description of the three rods I use for river flyfishing, carefully chosen and the product of many years trial and occasional error, may be of help – though I do not pretend that they would suit every angler or every fishing situation. By chance, they include all three of the main materials currently used for rod building.

The first is a delightful, somewhat stiff, 7-foot cane brook rod, rated #5. It is used markedly less than either of the others, but comes into its own on heavily overgrown streams in Devon where I like to wade up through arcades of trees, casting in beneath the banks and to gaps amongst the tree roots for trout which (I fondly imagine) go unharried for the rest of the year.

The second is an $8\frac{1}{2}$-foot, #6-rated fibreglass model that I have had for fifteen years now. It has a slightly soft, all-through action, and has served me well on the upper Bann in Northern Ireland, on the Usk, the Eamont, the Test, the Itchen, the Kennet and the Wylye, and on several much smaller chalk brooks in Hampshire and Wiltshire. It is an old friend and, unless I trap it in a car door or allow it to be munched by some mindless bullock (which heaven forbid!) I see no reason to replace it with anything more modern.

The third is a 10 foot, #6–7 carbon-fibre rod, made up for me for use on stillwaters some eight or ten years ago. With a medium to stiff, all-through action, I use it from the bank and from boats on lakes and reservoirs, large and small, and it is the mainstay of my stillwater armoury. But I have also used it to good effect in pursuit of trout and grayling on the Eden and for sea-trout fishing on the lower Test and on the Torridge. It is a delight to use and will very comfortably cast twenty-five yards of double-tapered #6 line accurately and without effort when called upon to do so.

FLY REELS

A good deal of nonsense has been written about fly reels – about the need for rapid line retrieval and the way in which a reel should 'balance' a rod. The truth of the matter is that a fly reel is no more than a receptacle for line

A fly reel should be filled to within ¼ inch of the edge of the drum.

that is not in use. The flyfisher does not cast from a fly reel as the coarse or sea angler does from a centre-pin, a fixed-spool or a multiplying reel, nor is it necessary to use the reel when playing a fish (although we shall discuss the merits and demerits of doing so in due course). And any talk of using the reel to bring the rod's centre of gravity back towards the angler's hand, presuming this to be beneficial, is just so much gobbledygook. (If you disbelieve me, work out fifteen yards or so of line, remove the reel from the rod and then carry on casting – you will find the rod noticeably more comfortable to handle without the reel than with it.)

So a fly reel is, to an extent a necessary evil, and the chief requirements of it are that it should be light and reliable and that it should be just large enough to accommodate the fly line and some fifty yards of backing.

Personally, I dislike multiplying and automatic reels, both of which seem to me to be unnecessarily heavy and too prone to mechanical failure. All of my reels are perfectly straightforward, single-action models, with ratchet checks, exposed rims (which facilitate the control of occasional maverick fish) and plenty of holes cut into the faces of the spools to allow the line and backing to dry reasonably quickly and to help reduce the overall weights of the reels.

BACKING LINE

Backing line is an item of the flyfisher's tackle whose purpose is often misunderstood, particularly by novices. Especially in river flyfishing, backing line does not serve as a reserve against the time when some leviathan of the deep vanishes across the horizon, stripping off the whole of your fly line. I can recall only two occasions in thirty-five years of flyfishing when I have been taken down to the backing by a trout. Both were on reservoirs, and in both instances the fish in question were foul-hooked. But backing line is important, nevertheless, serving to pad out the hard and usually quite small spindle of the reel, and thus reducing the extent to which the fly line develops 'memory coils' – the nasty, stiff, corkscrew effect that every fly line or length of nylon monofilament acquires if it is wrapped tightly round a small hard spool for any length of time.

Backing line should be waterproof, both to prevent it from swelling when wet and to inhibit rotting. Soft, braided nylon is ideal.

LEADERS

The leader (sometimes confusingly called a cast) is the length of nylon that connects the fly (and the fish) to the fly line. It is one of the most vital items of the flyfisher's tackle and one of the most often neglected. It must be so designed as to transmit power evenly from the fly line, rolling out neatly and delicately over the water, long enough to distance the fly from the potentially fish-frightening fly line, fine enough to go unnoticed by the trout and strong enough to withstand a fierce take or a charging run from an unexpectedly large fish. From all this, it must be evident that a single length of 4-, 6-, or 8-pound nylon will not suffice.

The ideal length for a leader for stream and river flyfishing is between nine and twelve feet. On small burns and brooks it may be necessary to come down to as little as seven feet because of the short distances being cast and the limited space available.

In order to transmit power from the fly line smoothly and efficiently right down to the fly, the butt end of the leader should be nearly as thick as the fly line as possible, certainly no less than half the fly line's diameter, and the taper should become progressively steeper towards the point.

Braided butts – consisting of from three to five feet of tapered, braided nylon – which have become available during the mid-1980s, are invaluable for the way in which they transfer a line's energy through to the leader, making it much easier to achieve a neat, delicate turnover and, thus, good fly presentation. A braided butt secured to a fly line should last for at least a full season without attention. At present (1987), the leaders that come attached to braided butts are somewhat arbitrary in both design and point strength, but it is a simple matter to replace them with ones properly matched to the type of fishing one is doing.

Commercially made knotless tapered leaders, available from tackle shops, are excellent, especially if a couple of feet of heavy (say, 25-pound) nylon monofilament is used as a 'butt length' between the fly line or braided butt and the knotless leader. If one is more economically minded, perfectly good leaders can be made up from lengths of nylon of various strengths.

Generally speaking, point strengths of leaders for river flyfishing are lighter than those used in stillwater trouting, partly because trout in running water are often smaller and tend neither to take so fiercely nor to run so far as those in lochs, lakes and reservoirs, and partly because trout in rivers – particularly those in clear-water streams – often seem to be more wary than those in stillwaters. A 3-pound (roughly 0·008 inch) point is probably about right for most river flyfishing, but it may be necessary to go down to 2 pounds when the fish are particularly shy or up to as much as 8–10 pounds (0·012–0·014 inch) when fishing for large sea trout. If in doubt, and especially if you are inexperienced, it is wise to err on the side of caution and to use a slightly heavier point, rather than one that is too light. There is nothing sporting in fishing too fine and then leaving hooks in fishes' mouths when they break us.

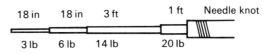

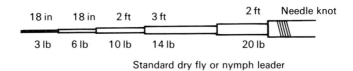

Small stream dry fly or nymph leader

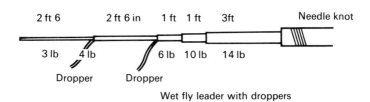

Standard dry fly or nymph leader

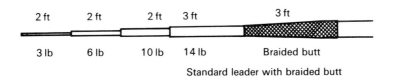

Standard leader with braided butt

Wet fly leader with droppers

Typical stream and river leaders

Droppers, used for wet-fly fishing, should be kept short and, where one is formed at a join between nylon of different strengths, it should be an extension of the stronger length.

FLIES

Last among our list of truly essential items of equipment are the flies themselves. Trout flies can be divided into three main groups – imitative and food-suggesting patterns; traditional and attractor patterns; and lures.

57

Imitative and food-suggesting patterns, traditional and attractor patterns and a lure. Top: olive nymph and hawthorn fly (both imitative); 2nd row: black & peacock spider and invicta (food suggesting); 3rd row: Alexandra and butcher (both traditional/attractor patterns) and; Bottom: black lure.

Imitative and food-suggesting patterns include all those designed to represent the various creatures that trout eat and those which, while not intended as specific imitations, look distinctly edible and are clearly taken by trout as food. Examples of truly imitative patterns include the Hawthorn Fly, the Deerstalker, the Cinnamon Sedge and the Midge Pupae. Some imitative patterns, such as the Pheasant Tail Nymph and the Gold-ribbed Hare's Ear, are used to deceive trout feeding on any one of an assortment of similar insects – the Pheasant Tail Nymph looks like the nymphs of many upwinged flies and the Gold-ribbed Hare's Ear is clearly taken as any one of several of the olives at the point of hatching.

The food suggesting-patterns are very often dressed as 'spiders', with a few, sparse strands of hackle fibre swept back around a similarly sparse body. Simple and deadly, many north country wet flies like the Poult Bloa and the Snipe and Purple come into this category.

Imitative and food-suggesting patterns may be designed to float, to sink or simply to subside into the surface film. Floating flies have long been called 'dry flies' and sinking ones 'wet flies'; for the purposes of this book, I shall refer to the third group as 'damp flies' – the Gold-ribbed Hare's Ear and the Hawthorn Fly are both good examples.

Although some writers have sought to associate some traditional and attractor patterns with specific items of the trout's diet, these dressings are not, in fact, designed to represent or suggest any particular creature or group of creatures that fish eat. Such flies (almost all 'wet') are effective chiefly because they seem to pander to the trout's innate curiosity or aggression, and they are quite heavily stereotyped, most of them being similar in appearance, especially in silhouette. They almost all have slim, cylindrical or cigar-shaped bodies, feather-fibre tails, beard hackles, and stylized wings made of rolled mallard or teal feather fibre or of quill slips and angled back over their bodies. Examples of such patterns which, on rivers, are mainly used for sea-trout fishing are the Butcher, the Dunkeld, the Mallard and Claret, the Peter Ross and the Teal and Silver.

Lures, much beloved by many stillwater flyfishers, are patterns dressed on long-shank or tandem hooks, not intended to suggest or represent any part of the trout's diet. They are rarely used on streams or rivers, except for sea-trout fishing.

THE PRIEST

If fish are to be killed for the table, a priest – a small club with which to administer the last rites – is an *essential* part of the angler's tackle. If a trout has obliged us by accepting our offering and coming to the net, the least we owe it is the courtesy of a rapid and humane release from its discomfort. It is wholly unacceptable to leave a fish flapping on the bank while we go in search of a stick or stone with which to bludgeon it to death, or to try to hold it in our hands while we beat it against a fence post or some similarly unsuitable object. The priest – which may be bought or home-made – should be secured to the fishing waistcoat or belt by a length of cord to prevent its being lost.

ACCESSORIES

Beyond these bare essentials – a rod, a reel, a fly line, a leader, a few flies and a priest – there lies a whole range of more or less useful bits and pieces with which the flyfisher may or may not wish to burden himself.

A landing net is not an essential part of the river flyfisher's equipment. Unless one is fishing from a high bank, it is usually perfectly possible to land any trout by grasping it firmly across its back, immediately behind its gills, or to beach a sea trout. But most anglers find landing nets useful.

A landing net for use on streams and rivers should be light and unobtrusive when not in use, readily accessible when we need it, reliable in operation and large enough to accommodate the biggest fish we may reasonably expect to catch. Except, perhaps, when sea trout fishing at night – when it may double as a wading staff – there is no place on a stream or river for one of the vast long-handled landing nets that reservoir flyfishers are so fond of sticking into the ground beside them. The net I use is of the folding-arm type. I sling it from a ring sewn high onto the back of the left shoulder of my fishing waistcoat – where I can get at it quickly and easily and where it is also well clear of brambles and barbed-wire fences – and it has never let me down. The American 'tennis racket' nets, slung on elasticated cord, are also good, particularly for small fish and for small-stream fishing.

Polaroid sunglasses are essential for those who fish clear-water streams. Cutting out glare from the water's surface, they help the angler to see into the water and, thus, to see fish. They also afford valuable protection for the eyes; a trout fly travelling back and forth past one's face at 30 or 40 m.p.h. is a very dangerous missile and, lodged in an eye, can do a great deal of damage. It is sensible to fit polaroid glasses with spectacle cords so that they may be left hanging on one's chest when not in use.

Fly boxes may be simple tobacco tins, smart, sophisticated aluminium jobs with spring-lid compartments and neat rows of clips, or anything in between. The choice is yours. But whatever you use must be pocketable. Great wooden 'suitcases' of flies should be left at home or in the car, serving only as repositories from which the small box or boxes in use may be replenished.

A small pair of blunt-nosed, serrated-edged scissors – available from most tackle shops – will prove invaluable. They can be hung from a 'zinger', one of those splendid little spring-loaded spools which can be pinned to a waistcoat and from which may be drawn 18 inches or so of cord with a clip on the end. Suspended thus, the scissors will be ready to hand but will not get in the way.

Used flies returned wet to the confines of a fly box are liable to rust and, indeed, to cause rust amongst others adjacent to them. A three- or four-inch-square patch of sheepskin pinned to shirt, pullover or waistcoat is ideal for holding them while they dry.

A few spare leaders or spools of nylon, a bottle of fly floatant, a tub of the powder now widely available for removing the moisture from dry flies, a small tin of Mucilin leader floatant (red tin, not green, which is petroleum-based and rots fly lines), a small tub of leader sinkant (made up at home from fuller's earth, glycerine and washing-up liquid, all mixed to a putty-like consistency), a marrow scoop and a small dish (for examining the stomach contents of trout) and, perhaps, a hook hone for sharpening hooks and an ordinary rubber eraser for straightening out nylon should complete the tackle of even the most comprehensively equipped flyfisher. And if that sounds a lot it can actually all be stored away in the pockets of or pinned onto a fishing waistcoat of quite modest capacity.

A sheepskin patch pinned to the jacket or fishing waistcoat is useful for drying flies. If they are returned wet to the fly box, they and their neighbours will be liable to rust.

CLOTHING

Clothes worn for flyfishing should be warm, comfortable, waterproof and, above all, unobtrusive to the fish. In all but the coldest weather, I generally wear a fishing waistcoat over a shirt or pullover. In its back pocket, I keep a very light and compact but fully waterproof nylon anorak.

When considering the colour and shade of clothing, it is important to take account of the kind of background against which you will be fishing. On open water, where the fish will see you against the sky, light grey or blue may be appropriate. Where you are likely to be fishing chiefly against a background of trees and bushes, mid- to dark brown or green will be more suitable. For grayling fishing on crisp autumn and winter days, I still wear an inelegant but highly practical camouflaged parachute jacket that I have had for years. It has plenty of large pockets to accommodate my bits and pieces, I have sewn a large landing net ring high onto the back of the left shoulder – as I have with my fishing waistcoat – and it serves me well.

A broad-brimmed hat is an almost essential part of the flyfisher's equipment. Apart from keeping one warm and helping to protect one's head from fast-moving flies, the brim shades the eyes from the sun and, with the help of polaroid glasses, makes seeing into the water very much easier.

Finally, waders should be reasonably robust and, most important, they should provide as secure a foothold as possible in the types of river you expect to fish. Those with cleated soles similar to the ones found on Wellington boots simply will not do when wet and slippery stones and rocks have to be negotiated; indeed, they can be positively dangerous. Felt soles are said to be much better, although I must confess that I have never used them. My personal preference is for waders with thick, semi-rigid, studded soles, which have proved safe on most surfaces.

5

TO CAST A

TROUT FLY

It is quite impossible to learn to cast well simply from the written word; there is much to be gained by going to a professional instructor. Indeed, many flyfishers who are self-taught or who have been taught by more or less competent friends would also benefit from the advice and assistance a good instructor can provide. Half a dozen half-hour sessions with a professional can achieve for a flyfisher what he might take almost as many years to learn on his own, and can greatly reduce the likelihood of his acquiring the familiar range of fundamental faults evidenced by so many self-taught anglers.

However, there are some people who are unable to obtain professional advice for one reason or another, and others who, while perhaps unwilling to seek instruction, may be prepared to look critically at their own casting and try to improve it. For these people, I believe it is worth considering the principles involved in casting a trout fly, pointing to some of the commonest casting faults and explaining how they may be corrected.

Our purpose in casting is to present our fly or flies to the trout accurately and delicately, over a reasonable distance when necessary, without undue effort. Effective casting has everything to do with timing and technique and nothing whatever to do with brute strength.

In coarse and sea fishing, anglers become accustomed to using their relatively stiff rods as levers with which to throw quite heavy terminal tackle (baited hooks, split shot or leads, floats, and so on) out over the water. A trout fly and the leader to which it is attached weigh virtually nothing and cannot be thrown any distance. So, in complete contrast to the way in which coarse and sea-fishing rods are used, we use a fly rod as a spring, loading it with the weight of the fly line so that it 'fires' the line, and the leader and fly attached to it, out over the water.

The mechanics involved are not unlike those we employed at school when we wadded up a piece of blotting paper, held it against the top of a ruler with our finger, pulled the ruler back to tension it and then released it, firing the blotting paper at the back of some unsuspecting colleague's neck. If this fundamental principle of the fly rod as a spring is accepted – as it must be if we are to get anywhere with our casting – then a number of other essential truths follow from it.

First, a fly rod cannot be expected to work efficiently without a reasonable amount of line out beyond the tip ring. Ten or twelve yards is the ideal to start with. Much less and you will have nothing to load the rod with.

Second, by far the greater part of the effort we put into casting must go into the *back cast* – to load the spring. Power for the forward cast must come very largely from the energy thus stored in the rod, rather than from the angler.

Third, the further the rod is taken back beyond the vertical on the back cast, the less efficiently will it work as a spring.

Fourth, the line must be given sufficient time to straighten out behind the angler on the back cast if it is to fully load the rod in preparation for the forward one.

THE OVERHEAD CAST

So, for a simple, straightforward, overhead cast, our aim is to extend at least ten yards of line beyond the rod tip, to lift it into a high, fast back cast, to stop the rod as near to the upright as we can, to pause to allow the line to straighten in the air behind us, loading the rod, and then to give the rod a forward tap, directing the line out over the water.

If you are a beginner, it will pay you to do your initial casting practice on grass, where you can concentrate on the job in hand without having half your attention diverted by the possibility of catching fish and where there is no water movement to complicate things for you. Instead of a fly, you should tie a small tuft of wool to the end of your leader. (If you tie nothing to the leader it will 'crackle' and knot quite unacceptably.)

Start by pulling about ten yards of line out beyond the rod tip. How you hold the rod is very largely a matter of personal choice. Grip it comfortably in the middle of the handle. Some people elect to have the 'V' between forefinger and thumb uppermost, others prefer to have the thumb on top. The grip one occasionally sees, with the index finger extended along the top of the handle, causes the rod to be held with the last three fingers, rather than chiefly with the index and middle ones, which is inefficient. Whatever grip you use, the butt of the rod should be tucked up quite tightly beneath your wrist.

For the moment, trap the line against the handle of the rod with your index finger.

How you position your feet is also a matter of choice to a large extent. The greater part of your casting from the bank on streams and rivers will be done from a kneeling position, anyway. But there is advantage in putting the right foot or knee forward if you are right-handed (the left for left-handers) as it helps to prevent the development of a 'throwing' action – by far the commonest characteristic of bad casting.

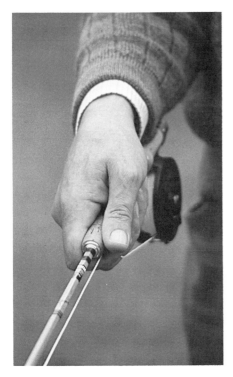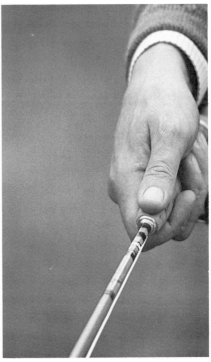

The conventional grips on the fly rod. Left – with the 'V' between forefinger and thumb uppermost; right – *with the thumb on top. Either is equally effective.*

Now, start the back cast with the rod tip close to the ground and lift the rod – quite slowly at first – beginning to speed up as you reach the 10 o'clock position and then flicking it to 12 o'clock, pushing the line up high and fast behind you. In terms of fore- and upper-arm movement, the action involved is not dissimilar to that used in preparing to throw a dart, with the hand being raised to the eye.

You should aim to stop the rod at 12 o'clock (it will inevitably drift back to about 1 o'clock, but must be allowed to go no further), and you should not allow the butt to break away from your wrist by more than about 1–1½ inches at the top of the back cast. (If you find this difficult at first, fasten a velcro-fastened cloth strap around your wrist and the butt of the rod.)

One of the most widespread casting faults is taking the rod too far back on the back cast, often because the butt is allowed to break far too far away from the wrist.

At the top of the back cast, *pause*, and do not be afraid to do so. If you have achieved a high, fast, back cast, you will be surprised at how long you can pause for without the slightest risk of the line or your fly sagging behind you – a full second, at least, with ten yards of line out. And you must pause, to allow the line to straighten in the air. If you do not, at best the rod will be under insufficient tension to enable you to execute a good forward cast and, at worst, you will crack your fly off.

Now, simply give the rod a forward tap, just as if you were throwing a dart at a board no more than ten feet away, and follow through, extending your arm slightly and pointing the rod at a spot three feet above your target.

THE OVERHEAD CAST

A *Starting with the rod tip low, and with the butt of the rod tucked up beneath the wrist, begin to lift the line from the water.*
B *Push the line up high and fast behind you; it is the back-cast that loads the rod.*
C Pause *at the 1 o'clock position to allow the line to straighten behind you.*
D *Tap the rod forward, aiming for a point two to three feet above the water.*
E *Follow through, allowing the line to roll out above the water.*

Perhaps the second most widespread casting fault is putting too much effort into the forward cast. A fly and fly line cannot be thrown. If you try to throw them you will decrease, rather than increase, your casting distance, the leader will land on the water in a heap and you will put knots into it – euphemistically called 'wind knots' but, in fact, always bad-casting knots.

For the most elementary of our river fishing, that is all that is required – ten yards of line, a steady lift, a flick to the vertical, a pause and a tap forward. But, for working the line out and in order to remove the moisture from a dry fly, it is necessary to be able to false cast. The basic movements are exactly the same as for a simple, single, overhead cast, except that line is drawn from the reel into the left hand and held there, to be released at the end of the forward cast – or in increasing amounts over a succession of forward casts.

For beginners, the interim step between a single cast and a series of false casts is to start once again with ten yards of line out beyond the rod tip. Pull five or six feet back through the butt ring of the rod and hold it lightly with the left hand so that the length from your hand to the butt ring is reasonably taut and the length from your hand to the reel is slack. The left hand should be kept by your side; it *must not* follow the rod up as you start the back cast.

Now, do a simple cast – steady lift, flick to the vertical, pause, tap forward – and, while you are following through, release the line with your left hand. Provided that you release it at the right time, the slack line will be pulled out through the rod rings by the weight of the line already beyond the tip ring. (If you release the line too early, you will hear a nasty hissing sound as you pull the rings down the line, rather than allow the line to glide out through them. If you release it too late, the power of the cast will have been dissipated and the slack line will not be pulled out.)

Your objective is to extend the line out over the water and then to allow it to drop gently onto the surface. If it splashes onto the water (or thumps onto the grass) or, less likely, if it is going out too high and then falling untidily back towards you, remind yourself to aim for a point two or three feet above the water's surface.

Incidentally, whenever you are casting – whether in practice or when you are actually fishing – you should always select a target to aim for; if there is no obvious fish to cast to, pick out a leaf, or a ripple, or a particular eddy, or even just a reflection on the surface, and aim at it. Only thus will you be able to cast consistently accurately when you need to.

When you are confident that you can extend five or six feet of line through the rod rings, you can go on to full, repetitive false casting. The action is exactly the same – lift, flick, pause when the rod is upright, tap forward, release line through the left hand. Now, though, you simply check the rod at about the 11 o'clock position on the forward cast and pause again, allowing the line to extend in front of you, before gripping it again and flicking the rod back into a second, third or fourth back cast.

Lift, flick back, *pause* . . . tap forward, release line, *pause* . . . re-grip line, flick back, *pause* . . . tap forward, and release line.

When extending line by false casting, it can only be released after the forward tap. If you try to release it at any other stage, it will go out of control and land in an embarrassing heap around your ears.

When fishing – and, indeed, in practice – it is important to remember that a fly line flickering back and forth through the air is very visible from beneath the water's surface and can easily alarm fish. False casting should therefore be kept to an absolute minimum. It is perfectly possible to extend fifteen or twenty yards of line with no more than three or four false casts, and your objective should be to do so.

THE SIDE CAST

This brings us quite naturally to the side cast – more difficult than the overhead cast but very much less likely to frighten fish, especially on clear-water streams.

We saw in Chapter 2 that light passing into water is refracted downwards, the extent to which it bends increasing as its angle of attack on the surface of the water becomes lower. As a consequence, objects on the bank seen from underwater appear to be shorter and fatter than they actually are, and something like a fishing rod held vertically becomes markedly more obvious than we might suspect – especially when waved back and forth, quite probably flashing in the light. However, if we cast in a horizontal plane, rather than a vertical one, the rod may well disappear below the edge of the fish's window and, even if it does not, will become far less visible from beneath the water.

The action of the side cast is almost exactly the same as that used for the overhead cast but with the rod held horizontally. The rod is raised slightly on the back cast in order to lift the line, lowered to the horizontal during the pause there and then tapped forward parallel with the ground or water. The two difficulties of the side cast are keeping the line high enough to avoid catching grass and other vegetation behind you, and achieving accuracy.

The solution to the first of these problems is to put a little more energy into the back cast and to angle it slightly upwards, flicking the line high and fast behind you. The answer to the second is less easy and chiefly has to do with practice. A rod moved back and forth in a vertical plane will, inevitably, deliver a line in the direction in which it is pointed, provided that there is no unduly fierce side wind. However, if a rod is moved to and fro in a horizontal plane, the line – and the fly attached to it – are as likely to swing off to left or right as they are to land where you want them to. I do not believe that side-casting accuracy can be taught through the written word; it is a matter of practice and perseverance. But the effort, if you are prepared to make it, should be amply rewarded by a significant increase in the number of fish you catch.

THE SIDE CAST

A *Raise the rod slightly on the back-cast and put just a little more energy into it than you would into an overhead cast.*

B Pause *with the rod at about 20° to avoid catching the ground behind you.*

THE ROLL CAST

The third type of cast essential to stream and river flyfishers is the roll cast, used both to extend line where trees or bushes behind you make a back cast impracticable and to bring an intermediate, a sinking or a sink-tip line to the surface so that it may be lifted into a normal back cast. The roll cast is simple to perform but can only be practised on water as it relies to a large extent on the surface tension for its successful execution.

C The forward tap is executed in an horizontal plane, which makes accuracy difficult to achieve.

D Aim for a point two to three feet above the water's surface as you follow through.

With ten yards or so of line on the water, lift the rod quite slowly to about the 1 o'clock position and tip it away from you by about 5°. There is no hurry in this phase of the cast; the object is to put the rod into a position where the line will hang down in a bow behind it before curving forward into or onto the water.

Now, bang the rod down hard towards the water in front of you with all the force you would use to hammer a nail into a board at waist level.

71

THE ROLL CAST

A *Lift the rod slowly to the 1 o'clock position, putting a bow into the line behind it.*

B *Drive the rod sharply downwards, as though you were banging a nail into a board in front of you.*

Initially, it takes a little courage to beat your (possibly new and precious) rod downwards in this way, but you will do it no harm and, assuming you apply enough force, the line should, apparently magically, lift back towards you and then roll out over the water. With a little practice, you should be able to put out ten yards or so of line quite accurately in this way.

Finally, do remember that the keys to good casting are timing, technique and an understanding of the mechanical principles involved, rather than the

C The line will roll out over the water and . . .

D . . . lay itself out neatly.

brute force and ignorance so often demonstrated by self-taught or badly taught anglers. Remember, too, that good fly casting does not come naturally, especially to those used to throwing things or casting with coarse or sea-fishing rods. Anyone can cast badly, lashing the water to a foam, half-hurling themselves into the river with each forward cast, accumulating a necklace of knots in their leaders as they do so. Effortless accuracy and delicacy come only with practice.

73

6

A MATTER OF

TIMING

Not unnaturally, the most consistently successful flyfishers are those who ensure that they are on the water when the fish are feeding. This may seem very obvious, but it is extraordinary how many people forget or ignore it, allowing themselves to succumb to domestic pressure to do this or that in the morning, simply grabbing a couple of hours at the riverside in the afternoon, or allowing dinner at 7.30 or 8 to drag them away before the evening rise.

Of course, it is up to each of us to decide where our priorities lie and to come to amicable and mutually acceptable agreements with our families as to when we may have leave of absence. But we must not expect consistent success if the timing of our fishing is dictated by human convenience rather than by the habits of our quarry.

And it is not only concern for others and personal convenience that can cause the stream or river flyfisher to sally forth at unproductive times. Those who come to running water from lakes and reservoirs often instinctively apply the timings they are used to on stillwaters to their new surroundings, but the two are, in fact, significantly different.

Through most of the season – certainly from May to September – stillwater trout tend to feed early and late, a graph of their activity rising steadily for the first couple of hours after dawn, falling away through the rest of the morning to a flat period in the afternoon and then (one hopes) rising steeply again during the last hour or so before darkness. Apart from the variations caused by major changes in the weather, this pattern is fairly consistent. Only at the beginning and end of the season may the fish be expected to feed, usually in quite short bursts of activity, throughout the day. As a consequence, keen stillwater flyfishers tend to be early risers, heading for the water at sun-up. But when they come to streams and rivers, they must learn to curb their impatience. Trout – and, indeed, grayling – in running water are more civilized creatures than their counterparts in lakes and reservoirs, rising late and rarely showing much interest in flies, natural or artificial, before mid-morning.

In fact, the behaviour patterns of trout in running water vary rather more throughout the season than do those of trout in stillwaters, and it is worth going through the season stage by stage to consider the changes in the fishes' movements and the factors that cause them. It should be emphasized, though, that these observations are somewhat general and that extremes of weather can alter the patterns or even postpone them for as much as two or three weeks.

EARLY SEASON

The opening date of the trout season varies quite widely throughout the British Isles, generally being earlier in the west (mid-February in Ireland, early to mid-March in Wales and the West Country) than in the east, where the river flyfisher has to wait until mid-April or even early May before he is allowed to cast a line. This disparity is caused partly by the west's rather milder winters and partly, perhaps, by the innate abilities of wild trout to regain condition after spawning, less commonly demonstrated by piscine populations often supplemented (and therefore 'confused') by stocking. Whatever the reasons, some of the best flyfishing of the year is to be had in March and April on spate rivers in Wales, the West Country and the north of England.

At this time of year, the successful flyfisher will be he who is prepared to cancel lunch. The two main fly species of interest to trout – and therefore to anglers – in March and April are the march brown (on larger spate rivers, chiefly in the north and west) and the ubiquitous large dark olive. Both appear, often in spectacular numbers, from about 11.30 in the morning until about 2 or 2.30 in the afternoon, but are almost completely absent at other times.

The march brown nymph shows a marked preference for well oxygenated water and hatches are usually quite localized, being confined to

75

fast, turbulent stretches of river and the areas immediately downstream of them. The large dark olive is less demanding and hatches can occur almost anywhere. But, early in the season, and especially on the chalk streams, it seems to be very temperature-dependent. In very cold weather, a slight softening of the air can trigger a hatch, as can a chill breeze springing up during a warm, muggy period. Under such conditions, hatches can be quite brief, lasting for no more than perhaps twenty minutes or so, but they can provide excellent sport when they do occur.

Towards the end of April, flyfishers in Scotland, Ireland and the north of England reap the benefits bestowed by the earliest stoneflies. The first to appear is the (generically named) large dark stonefly, hatches of which continue into June. I must confess to having almost no personal experience of early-season stonefly fishing, but friends who have say that the hatch itself, which occurs during the night, is of little interest to the trout and that it is the arrival of the egg-laying females on the water throughout the day and into the evening that arouses the fish.

In southern England, those favoured few whose rivers have grannom hatches will find the lost or late lunch phenomenon extending to the end of April. Unlike most sedges, this early season one is very much a middle-of-the-day creature, and so enthusiastically do the trout welcome her that it would be a foolish fisher indeed who would sooner be at home or in the pub than at the waterside when she appears.

On many streams and rivers, the last week in April and the first in May afford the only really good morning fishing of the year – provided by the hawthorn fly. Several fishing writers far more erudite than I have accused this terrestrial insect of being unreliable, both in its appearance and in its appeal to the fish. My own experience leads me to disagree entirely. The hawthorn, with its jet-black body and its gangling legs, has provided me with many marvellous mornings on rivers all over the country (as well as on numerous stillwaters). I suspect that most of those who regard it as unreliable do so because its season is so very short and because they arrive by the river late in the morning, when the fall is petering out. The last few days in April and the first few in May are the only ones in the season during which I make a conscientious effort to be on the water by 9 or 9.30, armed with half a dozen or so hawthorn flies.

MAY AND JUNE

The transformation seen on our streams and rivers between the end of April and the middle of May is astonishing. In the space of no more than a fortnight, problems of scarcity of fly life are replaced by those posed by superabundance, both in terms of the range of species available to the fish and of the numerical sizes of the hatches.

The large dark olive of spring is superseded by the medium olive throughout England and Scotland and by the olive upright in Scotland, Wales, Ireland and the north of England. Although the medium olive can appear at any time of day, my own impression is that it most commonly does so from mid- to late morning until mid-afternoon and then again around tea time. The olive upright is very much a creature of the evening.

May also sees the arrival of the iron blue, that tiny, dark, upwinged fly so beloved of fish and fishermen alike. It seems almost to relish the cold, squally showers we sometimes get at this time of year, hatches becoming increasingly prolific as the weather becomes fouler, great armadas of the little insects riding out the storm, providing rich pickings for hungry trout and sometimes, for tenacious fishermen under what often seem to be the most unpropitious conditions. Although hatches of iron blues are said to occur at any time of day, I do not recall having seen one myself before about 10.30 or 11 in the morning and, again, the best of them have generally been around lunch time and during the afternoons.

Milder mid-May days may see the first falls of that other useful terrestrial insect, the black gnat, and the first significant midge hatches should begin in the evenings – continuing throughout the season and, I suspect, causing some confusion amongst flyfishers who presume evening rises always to be to upwinged spinners or to sedges.

Especially on the chalk streams, but elsewhere, too, all this activity is largely eclipsed by the arrival of the mayfly in mid-May. So spectacular and fascinating is this phenomenon that it has been studied in detail and at length by every angling entomologist, and most flyfishers well understand its essential characteristics. (Extraordinarily, an argument still rumbles on between those who know the nymphal stage to last for a year and those who believe it to extend to two.)

The mayfly hatch proper starts in southern England quite precisely between 15 and 21 or 22 May, although a few individual duns may be seen as much as a week or more earlier. It continues until the second week in June, when it ends almost as abruptly as it began. The duns – large and wholly unmistakable – can appear on the water from about midday onwards but are generally most numerous in the mid- and late afternoon, and falls of the bright, shining spinners are most evident in the evenings, from about 6 o'clock.

It has been said, and it seems to be true, that the best of the mayfly fishing is to be had four days into the hatch, when the trout have had time to become used to the sheer size and quantity of the insects, and again a few days before the hatch ends.

During the mayfly season – and especially through the middle part of it – it is worth remembering that the other insect species are still hatching and that the trout can, and often will, turn to them as a 'side dish'. Only too often has one persisted with an artificial mayfly and wasted good fishing time in pursuit of a trout that eventually proved to be preoccupied with medium olives, iron blues or even midge pupae.

The end of the mayfly hatch sees a dramatic reduction in activity. Some chalk-stream anglers have attributed this to the trout having gorged themselves on mayflies, which is patently nonsense. The truth is that the vast majority of the surface flies that trout eat hatch in moderate to cool weather and are disinclined to do so, except in the evenings, in the high average temperatures of late June, July and August. Such daytime hatches as there may be from mid-June onwards tend to be sparse and spasmodic, thinly spread throughout the day, and, for the time being, determined morning and afternoon rises to hordes of surface flies are a thing of the past.

For all this, and for all the sad talk about the 'dog days', there is still a wide range of insects available to the fish and there are still fish to be had. But you may need to fish a nymph or even a deep-sunk shrimp through the day, and you may well have to cancel dinner in the evening.

Although the medium olive and the olive upright are still about (if in somewhat smaller numbers than hitherto), and the pale watery and the cinnamon sedge will have started to appear on the water in the late afternoons, hatches can be unreliable, and any expectation of consistent success must be reserved for the evenings, particularly for that magical hour around sunset. This rule continues throughout July and August.

JULY AND AUGUST

In his marvellous book *A Summer on the Test*, John Waller Hills placed July at the head of his list of favourite fishing months, chiefly because it provided him with the most exacting test of his skill. Newcomers to streams and rivers and those who cannot pick and choose when they will fish because of work and family commitments may disagree with him, for this is undoubtedly the most difficult time of year. These are the heavy, often humid days of high summer. The leaves on the trees have lost the lightness of spring and the undergrowth – thistles, nettles, cow parsley and brambles – are tall, dense, ensnaring and unforgiving. Streams and rivers are at their lowest, often with a languid lifelessness about them that can dent confidence even before we begin, and good bags of trout are hard to come by.

But it is a time, too, when experimentation, observation and opportunism can be richly rewarded. Occasional good fish taken against the odds can be far more satisfying than any number of easy ones.

In the daytime, we should not expect to see widespread hatches of flies with every fish in the river rising to them. Search, instead, for the odd maverick trout, tucked in beneath a bush and coming up to falling caterpillars or beetles. Spend time on the leviathan who has been lurking in the shade under a low bridge since the season began, often bypassed by anglers who branded him 'uncatchable' and concentrated their attentions on easier quarry. Try trundling a deep-sunk shrimp or nymph down long, deep runs or through the dark water of a hatch pool. Watch for falls of ants or black gnats and be prepared to take advantage of their often brief appearances. Experiment with a dry alder when the willow fly is on the water; it may well bring a fish up when all seemed lost. Look out for cinnamon sedges close against the reeds and rushes in the afternoons, and for individual trout showing interest in them. And wait for the evening.

There is something wonderfully gentle about an evening at the waterside in high summer. The air is often heavy and still, deadening all but the most local sounds. There is promise in the appearance of the first few pale wateries, blue winged olives, midges and sedges, and in the occasional early rise at 7 o'clock or so, which seems so certainly to presage a more general and productive one later on. Indeed it may, but it may forewarn of some of the most frustrating fishing imaginable, too. However sure we are that we know what the trout are feeding on, persuading them to take our copies can often be quite extraordinarily difficult on summer evenings. The answer (far from certain, but at least good for one's peace of mind, if not necessarily for the creel) is to keep calm, to avoid over-inflating our expectations and to watch the water very carefully, giving more credence to rise forms than to the often varied range of insects being borne down on the current. (The significance of the various types of rise form is considered on pages 83–85.)

Late in the evening, the fish are likely to be taking either spent spinners, midge pupae hanging right in the surface film, or sedges, and to be wholly preoccupied with one specific insect. The noisy, sometimes explosive rise to a sedge is usually self-explanatory, but rises to spinners and midge pupae can be very similar. If the trout consistently refuse your Lunn's Particular or Pheasant Tail spinner, try them with a small (size 14 or 16) Green or Black Midge Pupa.

SEPTEMBER

With its soft days, light breezes and excellent fly hatches, September compensates the flyfisher for the difficulties imposed on him in July and August. Sport can now be as good as it was in mid-May and, as the evenings draw in, we may go out in the daytime with reasonable expectations of success.

Pale wateries are likely to appear at any time from late morning onwards, as are medium olives and iron blue duns, last seen in quantity in the spring. And there may be some sedges about in the daytime, although the caperer, well imitated by William Lunn's artificial of the same name, is a creature of the evening, as are the blue-winged olive and its spinner, the sherry spinner.

OCTOBER, NOVEMBER AND DECEMBER

For those who extend their seasons into the autumn and early winter by going in pursuit of grayling, fly hatches and their timings become increasingly like those seen in March and April as October gives way to November. Large dark olives, last seen in large numbers in late April or early May, often reappear strongly throughout the country in October, usually in the early afternoons. The iron blue dun should still be much in evidence in October, particularly on cold, blustery days. And we may expect to see pale watery duns and spinners through until the beginning of November, chiefly in the late afternoons.

By mid-November, though, the flies of our streams and rivers will be drawing the curtains on the year, the nymphs becoming increasingly dormant and disinclined to hatch. Apart from very occasional flurries of activity on mild days and the odd hatch of midges, the insect life of the river will have put itself to bed for the winter, and we shall find ourselves compelled to rely on deep-sunk shrimp patterns and fancy dry flies, which may bring the fish up even when there are few if any naturals on the water.

7

DRY-FLY
FISHING

And so ('At last!' do I hear you cry?) we come to the heart of the matter – to the removal of trout from running water with an artificial fly.

Surrounded by mumbo-jumbo and mystique though it may seem to be, dry-fly fishing is, in fact, the simplest of all truly effective trouting techniques – in principle, at least. Essentially, all we have to do is to select an appropriate floating fly (being guided by those we see on the water or, better still, by those we see the fish feeding on), to cast it to a rising trout and to hook and land him when he takes it. The whole exercise is intensely visual and all the more rewarding for being so. But, while I shall be at pains not to complicate the matter, there is rather more to it than that.

Non-anglers often credit anglers with great patience and, perhaps equating patience with boredom, we almost as often deny that it has anything to do with flyfishing. But it has. Call it stealth, caution or careful observation if you will, the consistently successful dry-fly fisher spends far more time waiting and watching than he does actually casting.

And his caution starts before he even reaches the waterside.

The surest way to make absolutely certain that you will catch nothing at all is to show yourself to the fish. They are extremely shy and wary creatures, and they never lose their fear of man. So stealth is the keynote.

The successful dry flyfisher spends far more time waiting and watching than he does actually casting.

In dry-fly fishing – and, indeed, in all types of river flyfishing apart from the across-and-down technique – we start at the downstream end of the beat. By doing so, we put ourselves behind our quarry and enable ourselves to cast upstream to him, the purpose of which will become evident in due course.

If it is necessary to walk downstream in order to reach the bottom of the beat, do so very carefully, keeping as far back from the river as possible, using any cover that may be available and keeping low and moving slowly whenever you cannot avoid passing close to the water. Having arrived at the point at which you mean to start fishing, stop – and look. If you smoke a pipe, light it. If you can find a tree stump (or, on a smart fishery, a low bench) sit on it. Do anything to prevent yourself from cantering back upstream, casting at random with a fly pulled from the box on an impulse.

Watch the water. Look for flies on or above the surface and for rising fish. If you can see a fly – or, better still, a succession of similar flies – try to gauge their size and general colour and to match them with something similar from your fly box. With experience and practice, you should be able to spot and identify major hatches of duns or falls of spinners quite quickly (the tables at Appendix I will help) and to select a sensible artificial almost instinctively.

If there are several insect species on the water, or if you are unable to see any natural flies at all but the fish are rising none the less, the actual manner of their rising should provide you with some guidance as to what they are likely to be feeding on.

SUNK LURE

BLACK LURE

MUDDLER MINNOW

SURFACE LURE

DUNKELP

MEDICINE

SECRET WEAPON

ALEXANDRA

BUTCHER

INVICTA

PETER ROSS

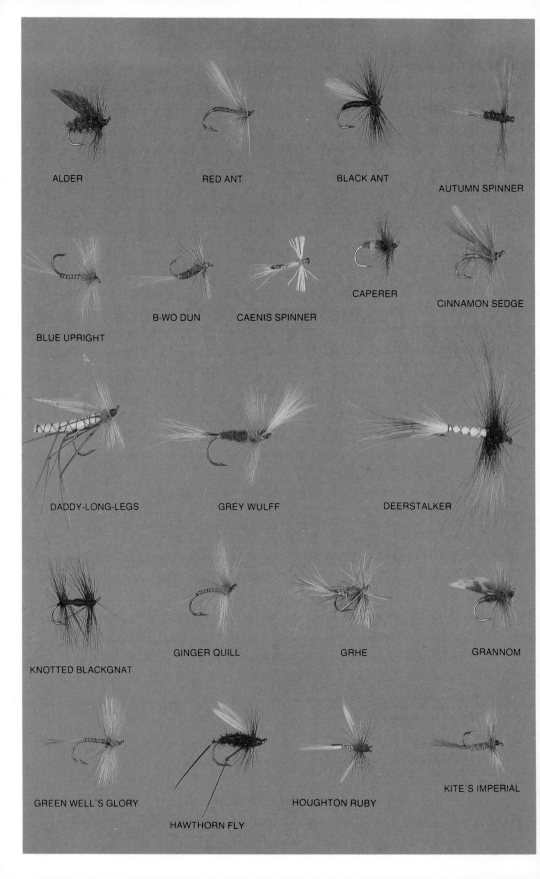

ALDER

RED ANT

BLACK ANT

AUTUMN SPINNER

BLUE UPRIGHT

B-WO DUN

CAENIS SPINNER

CAPERER

CINNAMON SEDGE

DADDY-LONG-LEGS

GREY WULFF

DEERSTALKER

KNOTTED BLACKGNAT

GINGER QUILL

GRHE

GRANNOM

GREEN WELL'S GLORY

HAWTHORN FLY

HOUGHTON RUBY

KITE'S IMPERIAL

The way in which a trout takes an item of food – inevitably displacing water, and often causing those familiar rings as he does so – is very largely dictated by the nature and behaviour of the food item itself. At extremes on the scale, if he is feeding on ascending nymphs a foot or so down, all the angler is likely to see on the surface is a slight bulge; and, in contrast, if he is taking big, active sedges, scuttling across the water in frantic attempts to get airborne, he will slash at them rather than allow them to escape.

A good deal of nonsense has been written about rise forms, especially by people seeking to show that a particular type of disturbance must inevitably show the trout to be feeding on a specific species of insect. There has long been a myth that a kidney-shaped whorl is necessarily symptomatic of a rise to the blue-winged olive and, more recently, it has been quite categorically stated that a head-and-tail rise is almost always the hallmark of fish feeding on midge pupae. 'Always' is as dangerous a word as 'never' when writing about fishing. There are too many variables – the speed of the current and the strength of the wind amongst them – for us ever to be able to be dogmatic on this subject. But it is certainly possible to identify perhaps five entirely different types of rise form and to use our understanding of them to help us to take an educated and intelligent guess as to the kind of food the fish are most likely to be feeding on.

THE BULGE

Whether they are scooping up snails, shrimps or sedge larvae from the river bed or working back and forth in pursuit of nymphs in and around weed beds, trout moving beneath the surface cause displacement of water. If the water is shallow enough, or if the trout is moving close enough to the top, the displacement will reach the surface and may be visible to the angler. At its most subtle, it may amount to nothing more than a slight 'rocking' of a mirror-like surface; at its most obvious, it may be seen as a strong bulge or swirl. In between these extremes, the 'stunning' of a small patch of slow-moving, wind rippled water or the very localized disruption of the natural and obvious flow of the current can also reveal the whereabouts of a fish feeding beneath the surface.

It is intriguing and instructive to watch fish behaving thus.

Trout twisting onto their sides in order to scoop shrimps and snails from the gravel on the river bed appear to have to use upward thrusts with their tails in order to push themselves downwards and forwards. In flat water less than about three feet deep, these thrusts can force quite a sizeable bulge to the surface, usually several feet downstream of where the fish is feeding.

Trout taking nymphs in mid-water may move sideways as much as three feet in order to intercept their quarry. They do this by turning their bodies across the stream and then giving themselves a push, turning quite gently back to head up into the stream and then sidling quietly back to their lies. It is the initial push that may create a surge of water strong enough to show at the surface, so the bulge will almost always indicate the position of the trout's lie, rather than the point at which he takes the nymph. This fact assumes particular significance when we are fishing a nymph rather than a dry fly. Very rarely can a trout feeding on sub aquatic food forms be tempted to take a floating artificial.

THE HEAD-AND-TAIL RISE

Unlike the bulge, the head-and-tail rise is one of the most obvious and identifiable rise forms on the river – and, to the beginner at least, potentially one of the most deceptive. That slow, lazy, languid porpoising, a head, a back and a tail appearing and disappearing in majestic succession, and gentle rings ebbing silently away on the current.

Think about it.

It is, in fact, the unhurried action of a confident fish, a fish moving to take creatures that cannot escape – such as midge pupae, the nymphs of upwinged flies preparing to hatch just beneath the surface, or drowned spinners or adult midges. Trout thus engaged can be some of the most persistent and consistent feeders in the river. They seem to get into an almost unbreakable rhythm. They can also be just as difficult to tempt with a dry fly as bulging fish can. But they are perfect candidates for the 'damp' fly – a Gold-ribbed Hare's Ear, a Hawthorn Fly, a Midge Pupa or even an Adult Midge, fished no more than half an inch or so beneath the surface. And, while such tactics may cause a little tooth sucking amongst just a few unreasoning purists, no thinking flyfisher would disallow them on even the driest dry-fly water.

THE SURFACE RISE

The surface rise is probably the most familiar of all, the one we hope and expect to see as we approach the river. It is faster than the head and tail and causes more disturbance – and it is almost always accompanied by a 'glop', the sound of a fish breaking the surface in order to take an insect floating on it. The surface rise is the classic rise of fish taking upwinged duns floating along, waiting for their wings to dry so that they may fly off – or, sometimes, black gnats, reeds smuts or daddy-long-legs.

Surface-rising trout usually lie no more than a foot or so down, watching the surface ahead of them and simply angling themselves upwards and giving themselves a slight push as they spot a fly approaching. Having taken their prey, they leave their mouths open for an instant to allow it to be washed back towards their gullets and to enable the air they have inevitably taken with it to vent through their gills. All of which is why, as we shall see, the flyfisher must pause before striking to a take to a dry fly if he is to avoid pulling his artificial out of the trout's mouth.

THE SLASH

A slashing rise often preceded by a visible bow-wave, is the hallmark either of an overexcited fish or of a fish taking a sizeable, escaping insect.

During the mayfly hatch (where it occurs) the trout, once they have become accustomed to the size and edibility of the insects and have realized that there is a surfeit of food being borne towards them on the current, can become almost playful, slashing at the duns with great ferocity. Later, during the summer's evenings, they behave in the same way out of necessity. Sedges scuttering across the surface in their efforts to get airborne present worthwhile but elusive targets, and the fish have to move quickly if they are to catch them.

Except during a hatch of mayfly – which will be blindingly obvious even to the complete novice – slashing rises are almost invariably a signal to tie on a bushy, buoyant sedge pattern.

THE SIP

Finally, that soft and gentle, late evening rise form, one of the subtlest of all, the sip. A brief kissing sound and a tiny ring of ripples dying fast, even on flat water.

This is the classic rise to the spent spinner, the female upwinged fly, her life's work completed, lying dead or dying on the surface film. The fish, well knowing that his quarry cannot escape, is able to take his time, nosing gently upwards and sipping each exhausted fly down quietly and delibera-tely. Very often occurring towards dusk, when the wind has dropped and the sun is low, the sip is not always as difficult a rise to spot as might be expected, but it can be deceptive. It is astonishing how very small a rise form a very big trout can make when it is feeding thus, and I have certainly been startled on more than one occasion when I have cast to what I thought to be fish of modest proportions only to find myself quite suddenly attached to three pounds or so of very angry brown trout.

So wait and watch, and try to establish what the fish are feeding on before starting to cast. And try to work out where the fish are, too – not just the obvious one rising like a metronome ten feet out from the bank thirty yards upstream of you, but the less evident ones as well.

In the next chapter, when we consider nymph fishing, I shall discuss the various ways in which you can improve your ability to see fish. In the meantime, suffice it to say that if you canter off in pursuit of one trout well ahead of you you will almost certainly startle others lying behind him which are very likely then to dart off upstream, alarming him as they do so.

It is impossible to overemphasize the stealth and caution needed as you move up the bank – and the slowness. Beginners have a marked tendency to be 'sucked upstream' by the sight of fish rising ahead of them, and when they fish with experienced and competent anglers they are often surprised at how long it takes to cover no more than a hundred yards or so of water properly.

I was given a graphic demonstration of this myself some years ago when fishing on the Kennet as a guest. My host and I arrived at the fishing hut at the same time as another member of the syndicate, a cheerful and charming man but a victim of polio, confined to a wheelchair. After a few minutes chat, he said he was happy to fish the short stretch of water close to the car park, and we headed off to beats further away. By the time we met up again for lunch, my host and I had covered a couple of hundred yards of water apiece and had each taken a brace of fish; our disabled companion had covered no more than twenty yards, had tucked half a dozen nice brown trout into his creel and was packing up to go home.

When you have identified the nearest fish worth casting to and are reasonably confident that you know what it is feeding on, work your way into a position from which you can reach it, keeping your silhouette low, moving slowly and using every available scrap of cover as you do so. Precisely how near you should try to get to the fish will depend upon the nature of the water and the bankside vegetation, and the extent to which you risk frightening him by approaching too close. Ten yards or so is the ideal, but you may have to get much nearer on a small burn or brook.

All your dry flies should have been treated with floatant at home and your leader *very lightly* greased to within two or three feet of the fly (but no closer) while you were putting your rod up.

Now, watch him again; reassure yourself that he is still unaware of your presence and study the rhythm of his rise. If he is coming up regularly – say, every 30 seconds – it will almost certainly pay to try to coincide the presentation of your artificial with a moment at which he may be expected to rise again anyway.

To minimize the risk of alerting your quarry, work out line over the bank or (better still) across the river behind him, rather than directly towards him, and then aim to drop the fly lightly onto the water's surface two or three feet upstream of him. If he does not take it, do not lift off and recast at once, but allow it to drift back well behind him before doing so.

A *Standing four-square on the sky-line, making not even the slightest concession to camouflage or concealment – the sure way to terrify trout.*
B *Well camouflaged and well concealed – essential if you are to approach to within casting range.*

The moment your line and leader are on the water, the current will take hold of them, carrying them back towards you. If you are to retain contact with your fly and to be able to strike effectively, you must start to shorten line at once. On a reasonably sedate stream or river, this is best achieved with a figure-of-eight retrieve, the line coming from the butt ring of the rod over the index finger of the rod hand (so that it may be trapped against the handle if necessary) and being bunched in the other hand. In faster water, it may be necessary to strip line back over the rod-hand index finger quite quickly or, if you are using a longish rod, simply to pull line down with the non-rod hand and to raise the rod tip as the fly comes towards you.

If the fish refuses your offering, do not give up and go charging off to find another, probably no more amenable than the first. Trout, particularly brown trout, are contrary creatures and may take an artificial at the tenth, twentieth or even thirtieth presentation, although the odds against rising them undoubtedly increase with each successive try.

It pays to 'rest' them quite frequently, watching again carefully to establish whether our original diagnoses of the fly on the water and the fish's rise form were correct, perhaps changing to a different pattern – either an alternative representation of the natural we believe him to be taking or a smaller version of the one we have been using. It is surprising how often stepping down a couple of hook sizes will elicit a take from a previously wholly uninterested trout. Occasionally, a fish will come up beneath our fly and drift back on the current scrutinizing it closely, with it almost balanced on his nose, eventually gliding nonchalantly back to his lie. When this happens, a reduction in fly size will very often provide the solution. Only when you are wholly convinced that you have put the fish down with your casting or that no pattern in your fly box has any chance of tempting him should you consider moving on (as cautiously as ever) to lay siege to your next potential victim.

DRAG

One of the commonest causes of a trout's refusal to co-operate with us in running water is drag – the unnatural, cross-current movement of our fly on the water caused by differences in the rate of flow at various points across the stream and by the effect of those variations on our line and leader. Drag may be very obvious, with the fly skidding across the surface at great speed, or it may be imperceptible. At either extreme, and at all points in between, trout hate it, and they will rarely have anything to do with a dragging dry fly.

A cross current cast. The rising fish was just below the protruding rocks, near the far bank. Drag is the dry flyfisher's most constant adversary.

Drag can be avoided in several ways.

The first is to position yourself as nearly directly behind the fish as possible, casting straight up across his back, but this method has a severe disadvantage in that the leader will drop onto the water immediately above and in front of the trout. A more effective technique is to cast to him from an angle with a slack or wavy line. This is not difficult to achieve. The trick is simply to check the line just before it drops onto the water, which pulls it back very slightly towards you. In most circumstances, this should enable the fly to drift down undisturbed while the current takes up the slack in the line. In faster water, it may be necessary to 'mend' line, flicking it into an upstream curve as soon as it has landed and mending it again as often as may be necessary. The problem with mending line is that it tends to skid the fly sideways across the current each time you do it, which may, of itself, alarm the fish.

Some fishing writers have advocated the deliberate casting of a 'shepherd's crook' – a sharp left- or right-handed curve in the leader – to avoid dropping the leader within the fish's field of view. This is quite easy to do, but my own experience suggests that the benefits accruing from it are almost always cancelled out by the loss of accuracy that seems to accompany the exercise.

So you have used your best endeavours to try to catch this first fish. You are reasonably confident that you have identified what he is (or was) feeding on and that the artificial you originally chose to match it was a sensible one. You have tried a smaller version of the same pattern and, subsequently, an alternative pattern to represent the same natural, and one or two others for good measure. You are fairly sure that the fly is not dragging as it approaches the fish and, anyway, you have been casting a slightly wavy line to eliminate drag or, at least, to reduce it to a minimum. And still he has shown no interest. Indeed, he has stopped rising and appears to be sulking a foot or so beneath the surface.

Give him best. Mark his position carefully so that you may have another go at him later (there is great satisfaction to be had from taking a trout that has resisted one's efforts perhaps over a number of days or even weeks), and move on cautiously to his colleague a little further upstream.

Check the new fish's behaviour carefully, once again trying to spot and identify the natural flies on the water and to analyse the trout's rise form. Check that your artificial matches the natural you believe the fish to be taking and that it is properly dry, so that it will float high and well cocked on the surface. Work yourself into a position from which you can cast to your quarry neatly and accurately, with the least risk of frightening him or allowing drag to alert him. Extend line either across the stream behind the fish or up the line of the bank and cast to him, aiming for a point two or three feet directly upstream of him and checking the line slightly just before it lands on the water, putting a wave into it to reduce the risk of drag. Start to retrieve with a deliberate figure-of-eight as the fly drifts down on the current.

In fast, streamy water on spate brooks and rivers, the trout's rise may be a quick, splashy affair. On more sedate, fertile waters, where surface food is borne down slowly, it is usually much more deliberate. In either case, it is intensely exciting for the flyfisher. One moment his offering is there, bobbing or drifting along on the current; the next it has gone, engulfed in a 'glop' and a whorl, and all that is left is a circular surge of waves pulsing outwards. Instinct tells us to strike at once but, if we do so, we risk pulling the hook from our hard-earned quarry's still-open mouth.

STRIKING AND PLAYING

The length of the pause before striking will be dictated by the speed of the rise which will, in turn, be dictated largely by the speed of the current. On calm, slow-flowing rivers, and even on quiet pools on faster ones, we may have to steel ourselves to observe the old rules of counting to three or saying 'God save the Queen' before lifting the rod tip. In rapid, streamy runs, we may have to tighten almost immediately.

I say 'tighten' rather than 'strike'. The word 'strike' has unnecessarily violent connotations. The action of setting the hook should be neither sharp nor violent. In fact, all that is required is to perform exactly the same movement you would use if you were going into a back cast, raising the rod and simply tightening on the fish.

Instinct impels most anglers to strike directly away from the fish. In fact, this is by no means always the most efficient way of setting the hook. If you are fishing across fairly rapid water, or if any of the line between your rod tip and the fly has drifted downstream of you (which you should have been seeking to prevent by retrieving line), it is better to strike upstream, against, rather than with, the pressure of the water. And, if you are using a fine leader point, it pays to release the line from your left hand momentarily as you strike. The friction of the rod rings on the line is usually quite sufficient to set the hook.

How a fish behaves when hooked will depend largely on the species and, to a lesser extent, on the character of the individual specimen. Brown trout tend to be dour and dogged, either heading for their chosen bolt-holes beneath a bank, amongst tree roots or in a weed bed, or engaging in a tug-of-war in deep water if they can reach it. Rainbow trout usually fight more spectacularly, quite often leaping from the water, but generally tiring more quickly than browns do.

Tighten, rather than strike. Richard Slocock responds to a rise on the Dorset Piddle.

If a fish is able to get downstream of the angler, both the angler and his tackle will have the weight of the current to contend with as well as the antics of the fish. This can pose quite serious problems in fast water, even with trout of only modest proportions, and it is as well to keep the fish upstream of you if you can.

The rod tip should be kept up throughout the playing of a fish. The springiness of the rod acts as a buffer, protecting the leader and the hook-hold in the fish's mouth from sudden fierce tugs and rushes. If the fish starts to pull the rod tip inexorably downwards, keep the tip up by allowing him to take line out; line thus released to him can always be retrieved later.

Whether you play a fish from the reel or simply by retrieving line through the rod rings and allowing it to fall onto the bank or into the water beside you is largely a matter for personal choice. There are arguments for and against both methods.

To play a fish from the reel is neat and tidy, and obviates the risk of treading on the line or having it snag on a thistle or a piece of tree root. But too many fish are lost by flyfishers more concerned with taking up slack line onto the reel as soon as a fish has been hooked rather than with concentrating on what the fish itself is doing. And the inertia of a fly reel can be sufficient to break the leader if an unusually large or active fish makes an unexpected lunge for freedom. On the other hand, line lying loose on the ground can easily be stepped on, tangle, or become caught around an obstruction, which can also cause breakage if the fish suddenly takes off.

If a trout does jump, the rod tip should be lowered briefly to minimize the risk of the leader being broken by the sudden jarring or by the fish falling back onto it.

Whether you choose to play the fish from the reel or by hand, your objective should be to keep him clear of hazards and to bring him to the net as quickly and efficiently as reasonably possible. Trout can be steered away from obstructions by the use of side strain – tipping the rod over until it is almost horizontal and thus applying lateral pressure. If a fish does bury itself in weed, light pressure will often extricate him. If this fails, try pointing the rod directly at him and then gently hand-lining him out. Incidentally, a fish thus extracted and blinded by a swathe of weed around his head will usually come to the net wholly inert, with no further fight at all, but this always seems to me to be rather a sad end to a sporting encounter.

Throughout the playing of a fish, the angler should keep low and use such cover as may be available, not only to avoid agitating the fish he has hooked but, just as important, to avoid alarming others he may wish to pursue once this one is safely on the bank. It is quite remarkable how very much more fiercely a trout will fight if he can see the angler and his net than if he cannot.

Keep low, use such cover as may be available and keep the rod tip up.

If a trout is to be released, the hook should be twisted free under water.

CAPTURE AND RELEASE OR DISPATCH

Once the fish has been played out he can either be released or netted and dispatched.

If you mean to set a trout free, he should be subdued as quickly as possible to avoid exhausting him and building up an accumulation of debilitating lactic acid in his muscle tissue, and he should be released in the water without being handled. This is easy to do if you are using barbless hooks, as you should be. You can simply run your hand down the leader, grasp the shank of the hook and gently twist it free without damaging the fish at all. Having done this, you should check that the fish is all right, if necessary holding him upright, facing into the current, until he is ready to swim off. Under no circumstances should a fish you intend to release be held with dry hands. Dry hands will remove the vitally protective mucous coating from its skin; their heat must be searing to a cold-blooded creature; and the pressure applied is likely to cause fatal (if not immediately evident) damage to the swim bladder and other internal organs. If a fish must be landed before release, lay him on damp grass or weed, wet your hands thoroughly and restrain him no more than absolutely necessary, just using your fingertips.

If a trout is to be killed for the table, wait until he is fully played out, place the net in the water, keep the rod tip up and draw him over the net. Never scoop at the fish with the net; to do so is an almost certain recipe for disaster as it will cause him to panic and bolt off again and you may well break the leader or pull the hook out in the process. If the fish is of modest

Wait until the fish is played out and then draw it over the net. Never scoop at it.

The fish should be dispatched at once, while still in the net, before the fly is removed.

proportions, he can simply be lifted from the water; if he is larger and there is any risk of his weight damaging the arms or frame of the landing net, it may be necessary to shorten your grip on the handle or even, in an extreme case, to drag it up the bank.

Once you have him ashore, the fish should be dispatched at once, as quickly and humanely as possible. *Before* removing him from the net or extracting the fly from his mouth, grasp him firmly across his back just behind the gills (the net will help you to obtain a secure grip), hold him upright and give him three or four sharp taps on the top of his head, immediately behind his eyes (being careful not to hit your thumb at the same time, says he from painful experience!). Properly done, this will kill him instantly, although his nerves may make him continue to twitch or flap for a minute or so – and you can now remove him from the net, free the hook and admire your catch.

If you are wading – a subject we shall consider in some detail in Chapter 9 – it is almost certainly better to secure the fish by hand rather than try to net him. This is easily done. When he is played out – and assuming that you do not mean to release him – draw him towards you and grasp him firmly across his back, immediately behind his gills. When you have a firm grip, tuck your rod under one arm or, better still, trap it under a short ($1\frac{1}{2}$ inches) velcro- or press-stud-fastened strap sewn onto the chest of your fishing waistcoat, leaving both hands free to dispatch the fish and remove the hook. Trout killed for the table while wading can be kept in a net (*not* a plastic bag, which will discolour them) or on a stringer – a length of cord which is passed in through one gill cover and out through the fish's mouth – slung from your belt.

Once you have released or dispatched your quarry, you should dry your fly thoroughly and tidy it up, and check that it is undamaged and securely fastened to the leader before starting to fish again. In fact, however thoroughly treated with floatant they may have been, and however carefully you dry them after the event, dry flies munched and dragged about in the water by trout rarely float well again until they have been given an hour or so in which to dry out properly. So it is usually sensible to tie on a new one when you have caught a fish or when the original has become too damp to float high on the water.

And that, in essence, is what dry-fly fishing is about. As the angler gains in experience, he or she will learn some of the variations on the theme that make it the intriguing and exciting sport it is – that the biggest and wiliest trout in any stream or river will almost always be in the most inaccessible places, under low bridges, tucked in beneath overhanging bushes, at the bottom of the deepest, darkest pools, or in virtually unreachable back-eddies; that the fish may well be feeding on something other than the most prolific and obvious species of fly on the water (who has not cursed trout picking out olives from amongst an armada of mayflies drifting down on the current?); that the evening rise can boost enthusiasm and confidence to quite unreasonable heights and, at the same time, provide some of the most rarefied frustration imaginable; and that the moment we begin to believe we have found the answers to particular problems new problems will appear to bemuse and confuse us.

8

THE UPSTREAM
NYMPH

Nymph fishing involves the presentation of imitations or representations of the immature underwater nymphal and pupal stages of a whole range of flies (and, sometimes, the presentation of shrimp patterns) to feeding trout in as realistic a manner as possible.

For all the contempt poured on it by those who fished the southern chalk streams in the late nineteenth and early twentieth centuries, nymph fishing is, in fact, the most testing form of the river or stream flyfisher's craft. It calls for exactly the same degree of caution, stealth, accuracy and delicacy as is required for effective dry-fly fishing and, in addition, it presents new problems of its own in terms of fish location, fly presentation and take detection.

LOCATING THE FISH

The most essential new skill needed by those who would progress from the dry fly to the nymph is the ability to see into the water -- to see fish and to identify takes when they occur. Fortunately, this ability is not simply a God-given talent. It can be cultivated and developed, and anybody with reasonable eyesight can become good at it with perseverance and practice.

*An eye shade or a broad brimmed hat will cut out extraneous light and
polaroid sunglasses will reduce glare from the water's surface.*

The first thing to do is to give your eyes as much physical help as you
can. An eye-shade or a broad-brimmed hat will cut out extraneous light,
and a good pair of polaroid sunglasses will reduce glare from the water's
surface to a minimum. Both of these aids are essential for successful nymph
fishing on clear-water streams. Having acquired them, you must learn
where to look and what to look for.

As we saw in Chapter 2, trout seek lies which provide them with cover
and protect them from the full force of the current but which still allow
them to take advantage of food borne down to them on the stream.
Obstructions in a river – weed beds, weirs, groynes, bridge piles, fallen trees

and branches, boulders, and so on – have areas of slack water immediately above and below them, the one at the upstream end being caused by the buffer effect of the obstruction and often quite deep, the one at the downstream end being sheltered by the obstruction and frequently relatively shallow. Trout take full advantage of these slack-water areas, but are more predictably to be found in the upstream buffer zones than in the downstream back-eddies.

They will also often lie in channels between weed beds, in which food will be funnelled towards them and from which they can slip into the weed itself when danger threatens or when they need respite from the current.

A string of trout is frequently to be found tight in against steep or undercut banks on the outsides of bends. Although the current is more powerful on the outside of a bend than on the inside, a steep bank produces drag which slows the stream a little, so the fish can lie in protected positions in narrow stretches of relatively sedate water and still gain access to the conveyor belt of food coming round the corner towards them. Such 'outside of the bend' fish tend to move only very short distances to intercept food, and to rise markedly more quickly than do their brethren lying in more placid areas, because of the speed at which insects are swept past them. It is worth remembering that when you are casting to trout in such lies your fly or nymph must be drifted round hard up against the bank, and that you will probably have to strike a little faster than you would expect to have to elsewhere on the river.

Although they rarely do so at other times in the year, trout will often take up lies in hollows or depressions in broad, gravelly flats in spring and early summer when their feeding urge is at its strongest, and they may return to them in September. Perhaps surprisingly, because they are out in the open, such fish can, in fact, be amongst the most difficult of all to spot.

Trout – often very big trout – greatly appreciate the shade and protection afforded by bridges and overhanging trees and bushes, and welcome as a bonus the various terrestrial creatures that are likely to fall into the water in such places. Lies like these can present the angler with severe problems of access and presentation, but it is well worth devoting time and effort to them for the disproportionately large fish they will occasionally yield.

The point at which two streams converge – usually producing an area of slack water at the foot of the 'V' where they join – will almost always provide a haven for a few fish, as will the small back-eddy bays found where culverts or ditches run into a stream or river.

Lastly, areas immediately downstream of cattle drinks, where cows and bullocks stir up the bottom, dislodging shrimps, nymphs and sedge larvae to be washed helplessly away, will very often hold some of the most

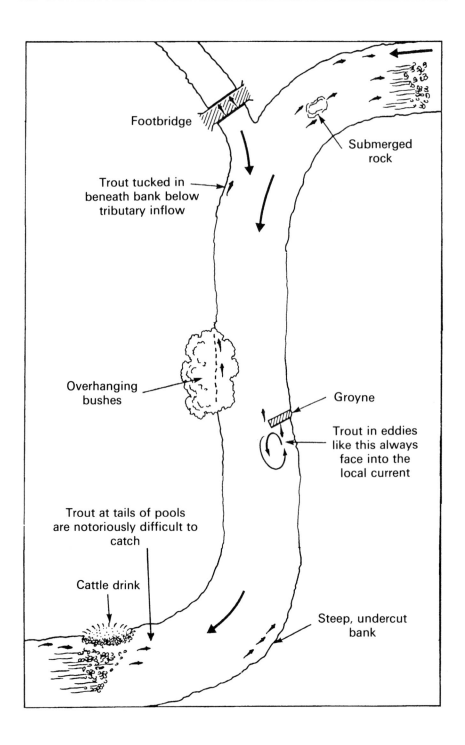

Likely lies in a typical stretch of spate river

opportunistic – and therefore some of the largest – trout in the river. As an aside, I have no reason to disbelieve the story of the experienced flyfisher who used to wade into the water at a cattle drink holding onto a cow's tail, using the animal to provide him with cover from which to cast to fish feeding downstream.

Having established the sorts of places in which trout may be expected to lie – immediately above and below obstructions, in channels between weed beds, tucked in against steep banks on outside bends, in hollows in gravel flats, beneath bridges and overhanging trees, at the points where streams converge or where ditches join them and downstream of cattle drinks – we must establish what it is we are looking for.

Trout and, to a lesser extent, grayling have an astonishing ability to blend with their backgrounds and can be remarkably difficult to see, especially against a gravel stream or river bed or when they are lying close to weed. The keys to spotting them are to learn to look *through* the water, rather than at it, and to look for *indications* of fish, rather than for the fish themselves, which will rarely be seen as complete entities.

Exactly as they were with dry-fly fishing, patience and slowness of movement are the keys to seeing trout and thus to successful nymph fishing. Those who charge up the river banks like beaters on a tiger shoot may well see fish – flickering off upstream in panic or scurrying for cover amongst the weed. But they will see none they can cast to with any expectation of success.

To start with, when you have worked yourself into a position by a pool or run where the light and the background reflected from the water's surface give you the best view into it, you may believe it to be devoid of life altogether. But as you watch very carefully you should start to see some of the tell-tale signs that will show you where the trout are – the upright trailing edge of a tail fin in an otherwise horizontally aligned world; a fishy shadow on the stream bed on a bright, sunny day; pale scrape marks where trout have brushed the gravel for prolonged periods with their tails; a bronze or silver flash deep down in a pool; a glimpse of white as a mouth opens and shuts on a nymph; or movement, the biggest give-away of all.

A fish that sidled into a weed bed as you approached may regain its confidence and slip back out into its lie. Another, otherwise invisible under a bush or beneath an overhanging bank, may show itself as it pushes across the current briefly to intercept an item of food and return to its cover. But most significant of all will be those that just materialize, having been there all the time. At one moment you are peering through the water at an apparently featureless stretch of gravel, then there seems to be something strange about it, just a hint of movement – perhaps a tail waving gently, out of synchronization with the weed near it – and the next moment there is a trout, vague and indistinct, but unquestionably a trout, breasting the current.

Having located a fish, the next decision we must take is what nymph pattern to present to it, and how. The former question is more easily resolved than the latter.

SELECTING AND PRESENTING THE NYMPH

Although it may be necessary to present a fair representation of the natural fly in terms of size, shape and colour when dry-fly fishing, we can meet virtually all of our nymphing requirements with no more than five or six patterns – the Pheasant Tail and Grey Goose nymphs cater for almost all the upwinged species (although I like to have an unweighted, general olive pattern in my box as well, as a back-up); a stonefly nymph is useful, especially on northern waters; a black or very dark olive midge pupa in sizes 14 to 18 is essential on most streams, particularly in the evenings; and a leaded shrimp or Killer Bug is useful as a reserve for deep-lying fish or for fish in positions to which the artificial must sink very quickly – immediately downstream of a dense bush, for example.

The problem of presentation is a more difficult one. When dry-fly fishing, we only have to place our fly accurately in two dimensions. In nymph fishing, we must work in three dimensions, seeking to put our artificial to the fish at the right depth as well as in the right place. To this end, the nymph fisherman generally casts upstream to fish, as he would with a dry fly, placing his artificial far enough ahead of his quarry for it to have sunk to the fish's depth by the time it reaches it.

In theory, the problem of computing the distance required for a nymph of uncertain weight to sink to a specific depth when attached to a leader of uncertain density and cast into a current of uncertain speed may seem wholly insoluble – especially when you can very rarely see the nymph or even be sure where it is once it has disappeared beneath the surface. In reality, though, it is remarkable how quickly one becomes quite adept at it with a little practice. In water of moderate pace, a size 12 or 14 Pheasant Tail or Grey Goose nymph sinks *about* a foot for every four or five feet travelled; a size 14 Killer Bug weighted with copper wire may sink 18 inches or so over the same distance, and a lead-weighted size 12 Killer Bug may go down as much as two or two and a half feet over the same four or five feet. Of course, 'moderate pace' is a very relative phrase, and much will depend upon the weight of the hook the fly is tied on and the amount of weight that has been incorporated into the dressing. But these rules of thumb should give the novice some idea as to how far upstream of a fish he must cast in order that his fly may reach his quarry at the right depth.

This computation of depth is important. In the previous chapter, I said that nymphing fish will rarely rise to take dry flies. Similarly, they rarely lift much above the level at which they are feeding to take nymphs, although a trout lying a foot above the bottom may sometimes go down to take a food item (or even an artificial) trundling towards him along the stream or river bed.

DETECTING THE TAKE

So we have located a nymphing fish, selected a pattern with which we believe we may secure his downfall and decided where we must put it in order that it may sink to his depth by the time it reaches him. Our next problem is to identify the precise moment at which he takes it so that we may hook him.

Many flyfishers seem unable to decide whether to watch the leader for signs of a take or whether to watch the fish. Personally, I have no doubt whatever that it pays to watch the fish, and the fish alone, if you can see him, and only to resort to watching the leader when the water is turbid or severely rippled, or when glare from the surface or overhanging bushes (or whatever) obstruct your view. The greatest mistake is to vacillate between the two, glancing from one to the other and, in all probability, failing to spot and correctly interpret the usually very subtle tell-tale signs provided by either.

If you can see the fish, watch it. If, when you believe your nymph to be close to him, he rises or falls a little in the water or pushes to one side or the other, or if you see the white of his mouth opening or closing, tighten, and tighten quickly. The pause before striking to a rise to a dry fly has no place in nymph fishing. A trout can take and reject an artificial nymph in an instant, and you cannot strike too fast. If you are fishing with a fine point to your leader – say, 3 pounds or less – it may be worth momentarily releasing the line with your left hand as you lift the rod tip or flick it out to one side. The friction of the rod rings on the line will be quite sufficient to set the hook; if you hold onto the line, there is a risk of breaking the leader.

Should the fish fail to take your nymph as it passes him, do not be in too great a hurry to lift it from the water and recast. It is extraordinary how often a trout will appear to take no notice of a nymph at all as it approaches him or when it reaches him, but then spin round and follow it for fifteen or twenty feet downstream before actually taking it.

With nymphs, as with dry flies, trout usually find drag off-putting, and you should aim to allow your artificial to drift down inert on the current, which is why we cast nymphs upstream and allow them to be carried back towards us. But the 'induced take' tactic, developed by Frank Sawyer and

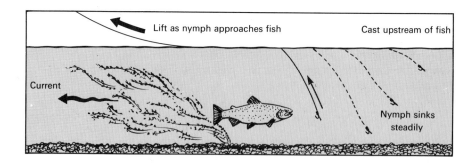

Lift as nymph approaches fish   Cast upstream of fish

Current

Nymph sinks
steadily

The induced take

given a good deal of publicity by his protégé Oliver Kite, can be deadly on occasions, both in persuading trout to take our offerings and as an aid to hooking fish in coloured water when we cannot see them.

There is nothing complicated or difficult about inducing a take. The nymph is simply cast upstream of the fish as usual, and, as it approaches him, the rod tip is raised, lifting the nymph up through the water. Whether fish believe nymphs behaving thus to be ascending to the surface to hatch or simply to be escaping, we shall never know, for nobody has yet found a means of interrogating trout. But what is certain is that they often find such behaviour irresistible, grabbing the offering fiercely and frequently hooking themselves in the process.

COLOURED WATER

So far we have only considered nymph fishing (and, indeed, dry-fly fishing) on clear-water streams, but this is not to suggest that either method cannot be highly effective on more turbid ones. Where a stream or river is coloured, fish location does become markedly more difficult, but this problem can largely be overcome by developing an ability to read the water (which craft we shall consider in some detail in the next chapter), and at least we have the advantage that the fish are less likely to see us – although that does not argue for our being any less cautious than we would on clearer waters.

When nymph fishing on coloured streams or rivers, we will generally be fishing the water, casting to likely lies, rather than to specific, seen, fish. While we may occasionally see a bulge in the water or a flash of bronze as a trout moves to our artificial, the surest way of detecting takes is to use a weighted nymph and to grease the top two thirds of the leader, watching it carefully as it drifts down towards us. If it checks or pulls forward, if it twitches off to one side, or if it suddenly seems to stop sinking when you expect it to continue to do so – strike, without pausing to wonder whether its change in behaviour has been caused by a fish or not.

This technique can also be used to good effect on clear-water streams, when light reflected from the surface prevents us from seeing the fish or when he is hidden from us by some other obstruction.

The induced take can also be useful when nymph fishing in coloured water, the rod being raised as the nymph drifts down past a likely lie, and offers the advantages that the take tends to be felt, rather than seen, and that the fish may well hook himself.

Non-anglers and those who have not fished a nymph sometimes marvel at the 'sixth sense' that nymph fishers seem to display – at what often appears to be an almost psychic ability to detect takes and to hook fish apparently wholly unaided by any evidence of piscine interest in their offerings. In truth, though, there is no magic involved. Concentration and careful observation are the keys to success and, with practice and experience, the nymph fisher's eyes and mind can become remarkably finely tuned to the subtlest movement in the water and to the slightest change in the leader's behaviour. Nymph fishing may, indeed, be the most testing form of flyfishing, but it is also undoubtedly one of the most effective and rewarding.

9

WET-FLY

FISHING

Dry-fly and nymph fishing can both be highly effective on most types of streams and rivers, on spate waters in the West Country, Wales, Scotland and Ireland as well as on the chalk and limestone streams of southern England and east Yorkshire. But, for reasons I do not pretend to understand and for which I have never heard any satisfactory explanation, they can be as unproductive on some rivers in Derbyshire and in the north – particularly in the north-east – as they are deadly elsewhere. Here, on rivers like the Nidd, the Ure, the Wharfe and the Swale, the wet fly reigns supreme, and its use has been refined to an art form no less elegant or skilful than that more widely associated with dry flies and nymphs.

Wet-fly fishing is as old as flyfishing itself, but its development as a specialized technique only really seems to have begun during the late eighteenth century, and it was not until W. C. Stewart's book *The Practical Angler* was published in 1857, followed in 1885 by T. E. Pritt's *Yorkshire Trout Flies*, that what is termed 'the north country wet-fly style' was formally encapsulated in print. Both books are now regarded as classics.

As a general rule, north country wet flies are tied as wingless 'spider' patterns on small hooks with short, slender, translucent bodies and soft, sparse hackles. Far from being fancy patterns, these tiny, delicate confections are used to represent a whole range of upwinged flies, sedges and stoneflies and to suggest all the various nymphal, pupal and adult stages in those insects' life-cycles.

In Scotland, Wales and the west of England, wet-fly fishing has evolved as a rather less imitative exercise. Here, quite heavily dressed traditional and attractor patterns similar to those used for sea-trout fishing – patterns like the Butcher, the Coachman, the Peter Ross, the Alder and the Invicta – are commonly used in pursuit of brown trout in often heather- and bracken-tinged spate rivers running from hills and moorland. But the techniques and tactics used in fishing them are identical to those employed in the north of England.

Wet-fly fishing is not hedged around with the (albeit pragmatic) restrictions that inhibit dry-fly and nymph fishers. The spider patterns rely on mobility for their success – both innate mobility furnished by the materials with which they are dressed and the mobility provided by the angler's manipulation of them in the water. Because they are fished beneath the surface, and because an element of drag often seems to make them more attractive to fish rather than less so, the constraints that compel the dry-fly or nymph angler to cast upstream do not apply in wet-fly fishing, and the wet-fly fisher is free to cast down, across or up the stream as he sees fit (though I shall shortly seek to show that upstream fishing, while a little more difficult, is usually more effective than fishing across and down is).

Because many of the rivers on which the wet fly works well tend to be coloured, it is rarely possible to locate non-surface-feeding fish visually, so the angler has to learn to read the water and to prospect for fish, moving faster than he would when fishing a dry fly or a nymph, and casting to likely lies. The chalk-stream guideline which expects that a fly should be put only to seen, feeding fish clearly ceases to be workable under these circumstances.

Ability to read the water is a highly refinable skill based on observation and on understanding of the fishes' behaviour. Experience and local knowledge help enormously. It is always good to be able to start fishing confident in the knowledge that there will be a decent trout in a particular run or by a particular groyne, that there should be a couple tucked in against this undercut bank, beneath that bush or amongst those tree roots. But even the relative beginner or the newcomer to a particular stream or river should be able to do passably well if he uses his eyes and applies a little logic and reasoning.

In the last chapter, I considered the kinds of places in which we may expect to find fish in clear-water streams. They will adopt precisely the same sorts of lies in coloured spate rivers, and what we must learn to do is to identify those lies from the visible evidence available to us.

107

WHERE THE TROUT LIE

A The buffer zones above or below an obstruction. This groyne is very obvious; some underwater obstructions may be identifiable only by the bulge they cause at the surface.

B A steep bank on the outside of a bend. A fine trout was hooked a few feet further up only moments after this photograph was taken.

C Overhanging trees and bushes provide shade and shelter for fish which will often be found to be feeding on the terrestrial insects that fall from them.

D Trout often lie in slack water just below the point at which a stream or ditch enters the main river.

E Trout are often found tucked tight in beneath the bank.

109

F *Good fish will frequently be found in the slack water at the tail of a pool, immediately above a stickle, but they are notoriously difficult to catch because of drag caused by the fast water below them.*

G *Trout will often lie downstream of cattle drinks, feeding on insects stirred up by the cows' hooves. The area around and below the fallen tree in this photograph would also be worthy of close study.*

H *Food concentrates in the fast stream that so often skirts a stickle, and the fish know it.*

Some will be no less obvious in coloured water than in clear. The buffer zones and sheltered areas above and below emergent obstructions (weirs, groynes, bridge piles, fallen trees, and so on); steep banks on the outsides of bends; the shade provided by trees, bushes and bridges; the points where streams join; and the sheltered back-eddies where culverts or ditches enter streams – all of these will be as evident to those who fish coloured streams as to those who fish clear ones, and all of them are likely to provide lies for trout.

It is only non-emergent features such as boulders, hollows in a gravel bottom and some weed beds that may not be immediately apparent, but even these may be locatable in reasonably shallow water or where they themselves lie not too far beneath the surface. Watch for tell-tale swirls, bulges and eddies and try to work out what causes them – almost inevitably an obstruction of some sort, and obstructions of all sorts provide lies for trout.

As important as being able to work out where trout are likely to be found is being able to tell at a glance where they will not be. Stickles – those shallow, bubbling, gravelly stretches between pools – rarely hold trout of any size or consequence, and should be bypassed quickly or simply used as approach routes to the pools above them where fish, often quite large ones, will usually be lying in the slack water immediately above the stickle, especially close in against the banks. For some reason best known to themselves, such trout are often particularly wary and difficult to approach, and it pays to creep up on them, keeping low and using every scrap of cover available. Putting a fly to them effectively is not always easy, either, as the line is almost inevitably picked up by the fast water at the head of the stickle as soon as it lands, dragging the fly rapidly downstream. But a little thought, care and stealth in such places will often be well rewarded.

So, although we may not be able to see the fish we shall be casting to, there are still usually plenty of visible clues as to where we may expect to find them – and where we may not.

Wet flies may be fished singly or in teams of two or, occasionally, three. The beginner may find it easiest to fish a single fly, which reduces the risk of tangles. But a team of flies does increase the angler's chances, especially when he is unsure of the depth at which the fish are feeding and the point fly can be worked deeper than the dropper or droppers.

What *does* offer an advantage when wet-fly fishing is a rod longer than those we would normally use for dry-fly or nymph fishing. Whether we are fishing across and down – in which case we may need to mend line quite frequently and to be able to lift considerable lengths of line from the water – or whether we are casting upstream – in which case the ability to maintain contact with our fly is of paramount importance – a rod of 10 feet or even more will make life markedly easier.

Which brings us to the question of whether we should fish upstream or across and down.

In purely mechanical terms, fishing across and down is easier than fishing upstream. Starting at the head of a pool or run, the angler casts across the stream and allows the current to do much of the rest of his work for him, swinging the line round until it is hanging almost directly downstream of him. He then retrieves only as much line as he must in order to be able to cast again and repeats the process, making his way slowly downstream as he does so.

Although it can be argued that the across-and-down method covers more water more quickly than the upstream one, I suspect that the real reason why so many people use it is simply that it is easy – which is really no justification for doing anything in flyfishing.

Starting at the top of a pool and working down it greatly increases the likelihood of the fish being alarmed by the angler or by the movement of his rod. It is worth remembering that, even in quite murky water, the trout, looking upwards towards the light, is likely to see very much more than we are, peering down into the water.

Casting across the current and allowing it to sweep the line round in a downstream arc makes it very difficult – indeed, virtually impossible – to fish our flies at any appreciable depth. Even with frequent mending of the line in relatively slow water, the point fly will rarely sink more than a foot or so and, as we saw when we were considering nymph fishing, trout feeding near the bottom will rarely come up in the water to take sunk flies passing above them.

And it is an indisputable fact that fishing across and down usually produces far more pulls and tugs than solid hookings, probably because we are striking upstream and therefore pulling the hook away from the fishes' mouths, rather than into them as we are when striking from a position downstream of our quarry. This is not only unproductive, it is potentially damaging to the fishery. The more often fish are pricked, the shyer they become, eventually, perhaps, becoming completely uncatchable.

So, for these three reasons – and although, as we shall see in a later chapter, across and down is an essential and effective means of fishing for sea trout at night – I firmly believe that for trout and grayling wet-fly fishing in the upstream style is by far the more useful technique. But that is a generalization, and we should always be conscious of the opportunism that wet-fly fishing allows for. There is no reason on earth why, while starting from the bottom of a beat and working up it, casting ahead of us as we go, we should not seize chances to put our flies to fish that may rise directly across the river from us or downstream of us.

Whether we present a fly to the fish 'dead drift', allowing it to sink and be carried down on the current with no imparted movement, whether we induce takes as we would with a nymph, whether we maintain just enough tension on the line to lift the fly and accelerate it slightly as it comes towards us or whether, in a slow running stream or pool, we allow it to sink an inch or so and then retrieve it quite quickly, as we might on a stillwater, depends entirely on the mood of the fish and on the types of natural flies they are feeding on. All of these techniques can be effective and, once again, the key to success lies in observation.

If there is no sign of trout feeding at the surface, or if the only sign is an occasional bulge, then we may reasonably assume (or hope) that, if they are feeding at all, it will be on nymphs near the stream or river bed or around weed beds or other underwater features. Under these circumstances, it is obviously sensible to allow our artificials to sink well down, and an induced take can be as effective with a wet fly as with a nymph. Because of their smallness and delicacy, wet flies cannot easily be weighted with lead as nymphs can be, but they can be dressed on relatively heavy hooks and it is perfectly possible to wind a couple of layers of fine copper wire onto the hook shank beneath the dressing, which can help. It is also sensible to degrease the leader very carefully with a mixture of fuller's earth, detergent and glycerine, and to check the fly line at the end of the forward cast so as to put a little slack into the leader, which will allow the fly to sink rather more

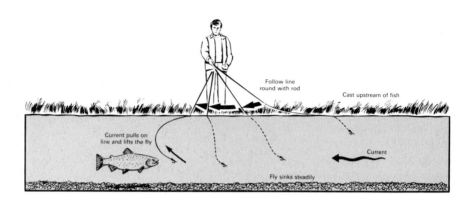

The leisenring lift

readily. Even when we take all these precautions, wet flies still tend to sink fairly slowly, and it may be necessary to cast quite a long way upstream of the point at which we believe a trout to be if we are to get our pattern down to the fish's depth, especially in fast water.

When trout or grayling are taking nymphs, an induced take with a wet fly is usually very much more effective than a dead drift, not just because the imparted movement is attractive to the fish but also because the movement itself 'streamlines' a spider pattern, drawing the soft hackle fibres down along the body of the fly, giving it a very nymph-like shape. The lift can be effected either by raising the rod tip as the fly comes downstream towards us – Frank Sawyer's classic induced take – or, when fishing across the stream or diagonally downstream, simply by checking the line and allowing the pressure of the current on it to accelerate the fly and lift it in the water – what is known as the 'Leisenring lift'.

When trout are bulging immediately below the surface or head-and-tailing, taking midge pupae or hatching nymphs, a modified and much more subtle form of the induced take can be deadly. Casting a short line to a point no more than three or four feet above the fish, immediately start drawing line down slowly through the butt ring and, at the same time, lift the rod to create a bow of line from the tip down onto the water eight to ten feet beyond it. The weight of the bow should be sufficient to draw the fly along just beneath the surface at a speed slightly greater than that of the

114

current. Apart from the fact that this style of presentation often proves almost irresistible to trout, it also almost guarantees that the angler will be closely in touch with his fly and makes hooking, if not a certainty, at least very much easier. And, if the fish does not take the fly, it is easy to lift off and recast to it again quickly, without false casting.

If the trout are surface-rising, taking duns floating down on the current or sipping down spinners, it is very tempting to put up a dry fly. Try it, by all means, and it will usually work in Wales and in the south-west, but it is extraordinary how often so apparently logical a step will fail on some spate rivers, especially in the north and north-east of England. When it does so, a wet fly fished 'dead drift' just beneath the surface will quite often provide the answer, the take being signalled by a swirl and, perhaps, a flash of bronze in the water, or by a sharp drawing of the fly line and leader. Since under these circumstances we are seeking to persuade the fish that our artificial is a drowned dun or spinner, and as the hackles of our flies presumably provide the illusion of outspread wings, it is as well to select patterns in which the hackles do stand out well from the bodies of the flies, and it is important that they should be allowed to drift down absolutely undisturbed so that the hackles will not be streamlined against their bodies.

A completely contrasting technique is needed to deal with a particular type of fish – an exceptional one and one which seems to defy normal logic, but one which is found often enough to be deserving of comment. He is usually rising confidently and fairly regularly in slack water or a back-eddy, often tucked in beneath a steep bank or an overhanging bush. For some reason known only to himself, neither inducement nor a gentle draw nor a dead drift will interest him at all. But try casting no more than a foot or so above him and then giving two or three sharp pulls on the line, from 12 to 18 inches each time, or just lift the rod tip quite quickly. It is remarkable how often he will bow-wave after the fly and grab it.

WADING

Wading may or may not be important to chalk-stream anglers – depending on the nature of the water and the rules of the fishery – but it is likely to be essential to those who fish spate rivers, particularly the larger ones. Many people enjoy wading and it can be very useful. The wading angler can often get into positions from which a cast can be made to otherwise inaccessible fish, and can sometimes approach fish that might otherwise have been unapproachable. Two gentle warnings need to be sounded, though. Careless wading can and does frighten fish and – especially in swollen or powerful rivers or where the river bed is rocky, muddy or contains deep holes – it can be dangerous.

For all the emphasis I have laid on stealth and caution, it is a fact that an angler standing in the water or moving slowly and deliberately in it seems to alarm far fewer trout than does his counterpart on the bank. No doubt his silhouette is lower and, strangely, trout do not seem to associate a static and detached pair of legs with danger. The two things that do startle them are the surge of water caused by fast or sudden movement and the crunching and clattering of clumsy footsteps.

So, if you decide to wade, do so slowly and deliberately, moving carefully and feeling for each foothold in turn. It will often pay you to ease yourself into a position from which you can reach the fish you are after and then wait for a couple of minutes to assure yourself that you have not disturbed him or, if you think you may have partially alerted him, to let him settle down again.

Avoiding alarming fish when wading is one thing, wading safely is another altogether. Each year, a small number of anglers come to grief while wading – most merely getting cold, wet and, perhaps, frightened, some making themselves quite seriously ill in the process and a few actually drowning. It is therefore important that every flyfisher should know, first, what he or she can and should do to reduce to a minimum the risk of overbalancing or being swept away and, second, what to do if the worst happens.

Falling in while wading can be caused by several things – slipping or stumbling on rocks or boulders, sliding down a shingle bank, catching one's foot in a tree root or some other underwater obstruction, sinking into the mud or simply wading out of one's depth and then panicking when a wader fills with water. But the commonest cause is an accumulation of events resulting from lack of thought and foresight. I have almost done it myself.

You climb into a powerful river at a suitably shallow point and wade out, being guided downstream by the shape of the rock or gravel bar on which you find yourself standing. Fine. Now turn round and try to make your way back upstream to get ashore. The weight of the current makes progress much more difficult, the bow-wave being pushed up in front of your waders pours in over the top of them and, before you know it, you are out of control.

Wading safely is largely a matter of foresight and preparation. Do make sure that your waders have soles that will provide a safe foothold on the most unforgiving river bed you may expect to encounter and, if you come across a bottom your waders cannot cope with, don't wade. Use a wading staff in all but the gentlest and most level-bedded rivers; it can serve both as a 'third leg' and to feel ahead of you for holes and other hazards. Examine the water carefully before you get into it; try to work out where you will

Wading is often necessary, but it must be done carefully and thoughtfully.

and will not be able to wade and try to work out where you will be able to get out, and how. (It is always easier and safer to wade upstream and then to move back downstream towards the bank than to be drawn into wading downstream and then have to move upstream to your exit point.) And, if you begin to suspect that you are getting into difficulties, don't just plough on in hope; stop, take stock, and work out a route to safety.

If despite these precautions you do fall in, *don't panic* – waders full of water are no heavier in water than empty ones are on dry land. Contrary to all the old wives' tales, they will not pull you under, although they may make it a little more difficult to swim. And *don't shout out* – expelling the air from your lungs which will help keep you afloat. *Don't worry* about your rod, your wading staff, your landing net or whatever.

Roll yourself over onto your back, turn yourself so that your head is upstream and your feet are downstream, spread your arms out and use your hands as paddles, both to help keep you afloat and to guide you gradually towards the bank.

Do not try to stand up and wade ashore as soon as the water is shallow enough for you to do so. As you climb out, the water in your waders will become heavier and heavier – on dry land, a pair of waders full of water is so heavy as to be almost immovable. So stay on your back until you are right in the shallows and then lift your legs up, emptying the water from your waders.

Let us hope, though, that no reader of this book ever has to test the validity of these emergency measures. With a little thought and reasonable care they should rarely if ever be called for. And we should certainly not allow the distant prospect of a possible ducking to detract from the pleasure of days spent wet-fly fishing on one of those lovely northern spate rivers, of wading cautiously upstream, casting to likely lies, watching for that swirl or flash of gold or for a pause in the fly line's progress as it comes back towards us on the stream, or of creeling a few of the fit, lean, beautifully marked wild brown trout that inhabit the waters that flow from the Pennines.

10
SEA-TROUT
FISHING

Of the three possible motives that may induce a fish to take an artificial fly – hunger, curiosity and aggression – the first is by far the strongest and most consistently predictable in non-migratory trout. For this reason, the emphasis in the last three chapters has been on the deception of brown and rainbow trout with specifically imitative or food-suggesting patterns. Now, when we come to consider the sea trout, we must revise that emphasis. While sea trout will quite often take some tempting natural fly or a passable imitation of it if the opportunity presents itself, they do not habitually feed in fresh water once they have been to sea, and they are essentially nocturnal. So we must use artificials which will appeal to urges other than the feeding one – curiosity and aggression – and we must fish chiefly at night.

WHEN AND WHERE

Although a few sea trout may appear in our rivers in May or even in late April, worthwhile runs do not generally start until June or July, and the fishing is at its best from midsummer until about September, tailing off as the season closes, usually at the end of October. Timings of sea-trout runs can vary significantly from one part of the country to another but, generally speaking, the first fish we see in any numbers are the school peal (or herling, finnock or sewin, depending on where you are). These first-run fish – weighing between about $\frac{3}{4}$ and 2 pounds apiece – are usually present in sufficient numbers to be worth fishing for by mid- to late June, most of the larger ones running from early August onwards.

Fresh-run sea trout, newly up from the sea, often carry sea lice just as salmon do – small, $\frac{1}{4}$-inch slipper-shaped parasites with two long slender tails each, which fasten themselves to their hosts' flanks in salt water. Sea lice are effectively harmless but serve to testify to a salmon or sea trout's freshness, dropping off when the fish has been in freshwater for a few days.

Sea trout are almost as notable for their wanderlust as for their shyness. Their purpose in running up from the sea is to find redds upon which they can spawn, and they push on upstream from pool to pool quite quickly when they can, often slithering up through shallow, fast-running stickles, their backs right out of the water as they do so. Spates encourage them to move faster than medium water conditions do, and in dry weather – especially in prolonged periods of drought – they will often remain in one pool for days or even weeks, becoming progressively more difficult to catch as time goes on. From the angler's point of view, this is significant in that a pool that fishes well one night will not necessarily do so the next if the fish have moved on upstream; even fish seen in a pool in daytime may no longer be there when we go forth in pursuit of them that night. Similarly, of course, a pool wholly devoid of fish one night may quite easily hold a good head the next.

Spates almost always seem to freshen the fish up. Sport is rarely good, especially with a fly, when a stream is high and coloured but is usually at its best as the water begins to clear and drop, deteriorating gradually – over a period of perhaps four or five days – if there is no further rainfall and the river falls away towards its minimum level.

RECONNAISSANCE

The prospect of night fishing may seem a daunting one to the inexperienced but – provided that you do not mind darkness, solitude and the almost always harmless sounds of the countryside at night (notwithstanding the occasional, unexpected bull), and that you prepare your tackle carefully before you set out – there is nothing particularly difficult or demanding about it. Especially on water with which you are unfamiliar, it pays to conduct a reconnaissance in daylight – ideally, during the morning or early afternoon, so as to give the fish plenty of time to settle down again before you start fishing later on.

It usually pays to conduct a reconnaissance of a sea trout pool in daylight, but it must be undertaken with the utmost stealth and caution.

Approach the water very, very cautiously. Sea trout are quite extraordinarily shy, and it is all too easy to startle one, his panic spreading almost instantly to the other fish in the pool. Crawl up to the river bank using every scrap of cover available. In a clear-water stream or river, you may see the fish you will be casting to tonight. Especially in bright weather, they will probably be lying in quite close-packed shoals in relatively slack water in the shade provided by overhanging trees or bushes, often quite close to the head of the pool, moving very little. It is worth remembering that as darkness falls and they 'wake up' they will probably spread out and, if they do not start to run on up the river, quite a number of them – often the larger ones – will be likely to drop back, taking up lies in the quiet water at the tail of the pool.

Check points of access to the water for hazards or obstructions, see where you will and will not be able to wade (if you believe it will be absolutely necessary to do so; you should avoid wading for sea trout at night altogether if you possibly can), and examine the back-cast area carefully for potential snags – trees, bushes, barbed-wire fences, and so on. It is worth actually trying a few casts across the river and tying a piece of cotton tightly around your fly line where it passes through your left hand when your fly is landing a foot or so from the far bank. This will act as a marker in the darkness and is an almost foolproof way of casting right across a pool without risking becoming caught up in the vegetation on the far side. If

121

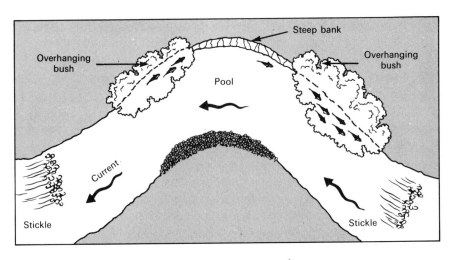

Likely daytime sea trout lies

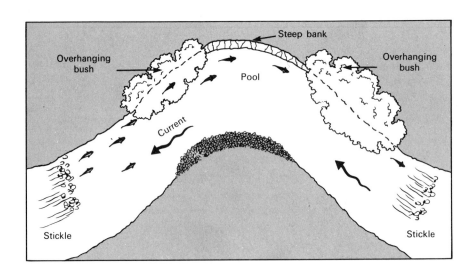

Likely night-time sea trout lies

you plan to fish in two or three places during the night, there is no reason why you should not put two or three markers onto the line, assuming that you can remember which one serves which fishing station.

It is important to disturb the water as little as possible during your reconnaissance. If you think it necessary to try a few casts, your exploratory visit should be conducted during the morning before your expedition, rather than in the afternoon or evenings, to give the fish plenty of time to settle down again.

On most rivers, particularly when they hold plenty of fish, a single pool should be sufficient to keep you occupied throughout the night. If the sea trout are uncooperative in the stretch of water you have chosen, it is very unlikely that they will be any more obliging elsewhere. But there is never any harm in at least taking a look at a second pool and even a third one, if only because a change of surroundings at two or three in the morning can so often restore flagging enthusiasm and confidence.

TACKLE AND FLIES

The keys to carefree night fishing are to carry the smallest possible number of bits and pieces, to know exactly where everything is and to reduce knot tying to a minimum or, ideally, to eliminate it altogether.

Effective fly patterns for sea trout vary enormously and apparently inexplicably from one part of the country to another – from Hugh Falkus's famous, large and sparsely dressed Medicine and sunk lure, and his surface lure, all so deadly on northern rivers, through the more traditional, size 8 to 12 Alexandras, Peter Rosses, Dunkelds and Invictas that are so popular on streams in Wales and the south-west, to the big, bushy, tandem Black Lures that are standard panaceas on the lower reaches of the southern chalk streams. When sea-trout fishing, it always pays to seek informed local advice about fly patterns, and to heed it, however much it may seem to be at variance with one's experience elsewhere.

Set up your rods at home or in your hotel. If you expect to use both a floating and a sinking or sink-tip line, it is sensible to put up two rods, rather than have to fiddle around changing lines at one o'clock in the morning. Tie your first choice of floating and sinking patterns to leaders and attach the leaders to the floating and sinking lines with loop-to-loop joins (see Appendix III). Make up spare leaders with each of your first choice patterns on them to cater for emergencies, and with such second and third choice patterns as you may deem necessary, and tie large (3-inch) loops into the butts of these leaders before winding them individually around a piece of stout cardboard from which you can readily free them when they are needed.

Some experienced sea-trout anglers fish wet flies in teams of two or three. I am far from convinced that this offers any real advantage over single flies, and it greatly increases the risk of tangling, especially for the novice.

If the water you plan to fish is not too hedged about with trees and bushes, it is better to use a long (9½ foot upwards) rod than a shorter one. A long rod will make casting easier, give you better control over your line – enabling you to mend it more easily when necessary – simplify the playing of (often very energetic) fish and reduce the amount of line you have to retrieve before lifting off to recast.

Leaders for sea-trout fishing need to be very much stronger than those used for brown trout or grayling because our quarry tends to be larger, to take more fiercely and to be markedly more acrobatic when hooked. Eight-pound points are by no means too heavy, even when fishing for school peal, and it is as well to go up to ten pounds when larger fish are likely to be encountered.

Ideally, if you have sufficient leaders made up in advance and if you know where all your tackle is, you should never need a torch when sea-trout fishing at night, but it is as well to take one 'just in case'. By far the best are those with flexible 'necks', which can be clipped to a fishing jacket or waistcoat and which cast a bright but concentrated beam of light.

FISHING IN EARNEST

When all is ready, and as dusk is falling, head for the waterside, but do not be in too great a hurry to start fishing. You are most unlikely to take anything at all until the last rays of the setting sun have given way to total darkness, and if you start casting too early there is a real chance that you will alarm the fish, putting them down and spoiling your first couple of hours sport – often the most productive ones.

So enjoy the sunset and study the water. There are few greater pleasures than to sit by an attractive river in lovely surroundings, watching and listening to the wildlife around you as the stars come out in a darkening sky. And twenty minutes or half an hour spent accustoming your eyes to the darkness is always time well spent.

A dark sky is a great asset. If you can pick and choose when you go out, try to select nights when the moon will be no more than a sliver or when it will be obscured by cloud. A full, bright moon can be death to sea-trout fishing, particularly if the angler has no alternative but to put himself between it and the fish.

If you really cannot resist the temptation to start casting before it is fully dark, then try your second-choice pool or, better still, a third-choice one.

There is always the possibility that you may pick up a few brown trout or even, just possibly, a salmon. But at all costs resist the temptation to start flogging away at the water you mean to fish through the night.

When darkness has fallen, you can start fishing in earnest, but do so cautiously. Start at the head of the pool, a few yards back from the water, and put out enough line to cover no more than a third to a half of the river at an angle of about 45° downstream, allowing the line to swing gently round on the current until it is hanging almost directly below you before lifting off and recasting. Sea trout that may have been lying in quite tight shoals in the shade or in cover provided by steep banks in daylight will probably have spread out during the evening, and there is no point in alarming fish close to you by hurling your initial casts at the far bank, thrashing your line down on top of them. And, if you cast too directly across the stream, the line will usually be carried round on the current at breakneck speed, skidding the fly along just beneath the surface behind it.

I usually start with a floating line and a reasonably large (size 8) traditional wet pattern – a Butcher, a Dunkeld, or perhaps Hugh Falkus's Medicine – except when I am fishing on one of the southern chalk streams, where a large black lure on a slow- or medium-sinking line is generally more effective than anything else throughout the night.

As you lengthen your cast diagonally downstream towards the far bank, the need to mend line will probably increase. Your aim should be to allow

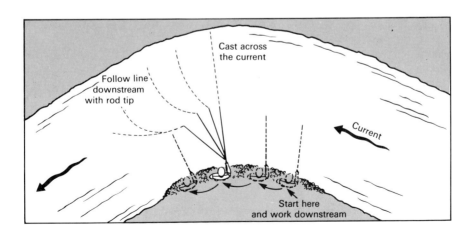

Fishing across and down

125

the fly to sink quickly and then to work it across the current quite slowly, maintaining its depth as far as possible. To this end, you should mend a floating line as soon as it hits the water, flicking un upstream curve into it, to give the fly time to sink, feel for the weight of the stream on the line and mend line again as and when necessary.

A useful alternative to mending line is to slip it – a technique I have not heard or seen described elsewhere but one that has stood me in good stead on numerous occasions and one which works as well with a sinking line as with a floater. The trick is to pull between five and ten yards or so of line off the reel in addition to the amount you mean to cast. Then, once the cast has been made, some or all of the extra line can be slipped gradually and evenly through the fingers of the non–rod hand, being pulled out by the weight of the current and serving to slow the fly's passage across the stream. As well as being an effective alternative to mending line, slipping line can enable you to fish a pool – or a large part of it – without actually moving, and to fish water that might otherwise have been inaccessible because of obstructions. The only problem is that as line length increases so does the difficulty of hooking fish, particularly when the fly has only just started to move across the stream and there is a substantial curve in the line.

Keep the rod tip low but do not point it directly down the line. Instead, hold it at an angle to the line and use it as a shock absorber to cushion the

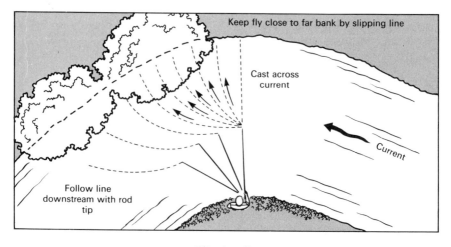

Slipping line

leader against the sudden impact of an often fierce take. A sea trout's take may be felt as a gentle pull or as a ferocious, explosive yank on the line, the fish erupting from the water in a cloud of spray. Between these two extremes is the frustrating tap-tapping caused by fish plucking at the fly rather than taking it properly; possible cures are to change to a smaller fly or to one, like Hugh Falkus's Secret Weapon, with a small bare single, double or treble hook protruding behind it.

However the take comes, get your rod tip up quickly, keep your fingers clear of the reel handle and be prepared to allow the fish to take out line – possibly all of it. Until they have hooked a few sea trout, most flyfishers wholly fail to appreciate the extraordinary power of these fish. Even a modest school peal of a pound or so can tear off downstream at astonishing speed, stripping line from the reel and turning only reluctantly at the tail of the pool – if, indeed, he does so at all – before dashing off again in whatever direction takes his fancy.

The principles of playing and landing sea trout are exactly the same as those for playing and landing brown or rainbow trout but the process is usually made tenser by the ferocity of our quarry and by the darkness, which often makes it difficult to tell where the fish is or what he is doing. Try to keep him under control as far as you can and use as much pressure as you may within the limits imposed by your tackle to bring him to the net as quickly as possible.

When you have netted or beached him, dispatch him quickly and humanely and put him somewhere safe. Especially in the West Country, but in other places too, that nocturnal pest the feral mink is now so common and determined as to present real problems. Fishing on the Torridge at night, I have had a sea trout stolen from the bank no more than ten yards from me, and a friend of mine lost a confrontation with a particularly fearless and tenacious mink which decided to take possession of a fish he had left on a shingle beach by the Taw. The safest answer is to put your catch into a fish bass (*not* a plastic bag) and to hang it from the branch of a tree or, if none is available, from a gate or fence post.

If, after a couple of hours, I have had no response to the wet fly on the floating line, or if the fish stop taking, I usually change to a sinking or sink-tip line and a tandem lure, replacing the leader on the floating line with one with a surface lure attached – Hugh Falkus's Wake Fly or a well greased Muddler Minnow – against the likelihood that I may wish to use it later on.

It is at this point that so many inexperienced sea-trout anglers give up and potter off to bed. They are usually doing themselves a disservice. While sport during the dog watches is not always as spectacular as it can be during the first couple of hours of darkness, it can often offer the chance of a really big fish or two. As I change from the floating line to the sinker, I sometimes

127

move to my second-choice pool as well, both to rest the one I have been fishing and to give myself a change of scenery and to boost my confidence.

The lure should be fished close to the bottom in exactly the same way and at very much the same speed as the wet fly was, with line being slipped to control and slow the progress of the fly down and across the stream. Now, though, it will often pay to retrieve the lure until there is no more than four or five feet of line beyond the rod tip, rather than to simply lift off and recast as soon as it has crossed the current. The retrieve, in staccato pulls, will quite often elicit a response from a fish that may have been wholly indifferent to a fly drawn across the stream in front of him.

If the tandem lure produces no response, the surface one may. Any reasonably large, buoyant pattern will do, but the technique for fishing it is entirely different from that used for a wet fly or a tandem lure. This time, it is the skittering commotion made by the fly's passage across the surface that attracts the fish, rather than the fly itself, so we must fish it quite quickly.

Instead of casting at an angle downstream, we can cast more directly across the pool, allowing the current to catch the line and drag the fly round, and there will usually be no need to mend or slip line. Takes to fast-fished surface lures can be the most ferocious of all, and it is important to keep the rod at an angle of between 45° and 90° to the line in order to cushion the shock.

So, tired and weary, the sea-trout angler makes his way home at first light, hopefully weighed down by a respectable bag of peal and, perhaps, one or two larger fish. Those who are able to spend several successive nights sea-trout fishing during the summer tend to turn the clock on its head, sleeping through the mornings and heading off to the river as darkness falls. And this is as it should be. But, although I have made much of the nocturnal habits of sea trout and of the need to match our hours to theirs, it is in fact possible to take these wary fish by day. Indeed, as I said in the Introduction, most people who have fished for brown trout on sea-trout rivers with any regularity will have caught a few peal almost by accident. I have certainly had several on the Torridge when fishing a dry size 14 Blue Upright for that lovely river's delightful if diminutive wild brownies.

DAYLIGHT FISHING

The problems associated with daylight fishing for sea trout in streams and rivers must be obvious and have to do chiefly with the fishes' quite extraordinary shyness, which argues for the use of long leaders with fine (2-pound) points. And fine points, of themselves, create problems with fish that fight so fiercely; even with a sensitively handled soft-actioned rod, breakages can and will occur when we find ourselves attached to sea trout

Sea trout are the shyest fish in our rivers. They should always be approached very warily, especially in daylight.

cartwheeling and somersaulting around a pool, charging off downstream and dashing back up again.

My own (somewhat limited) experience suggests that sea trout are most easily caught in daylight after a short period of drought, when they have been in a pool for long enough to have become accustomed to their surroundings but not for so long as to have become stale.

If I have emphasized the need for stealth and caution throughout this book, I would re-emphasize it here. Even when they have been in one place for a week or more, sea trout are still desperately nervous and edgy; the first careless clump on the bank or on the river bed, the first glimpse of human movement, the first flickering of a shiny fly line over them or the first splash of a clumsy cast will spread panic throughout the pool.

With a fine, carefully degreased leader of between 14 and 16 feet and either a tiny dry fly or – probably better still – a little traditional wet pattern (size 12 Dunkelds and Invictas have occasionally worked for me), creep into

129

position directly behind the fish and cast to them with all the accuracy and delicacy you can muster. If the water is clear and you can identify the tail fish in a shoal, cast to them first rather than line them by casting to larger fish further up. If you elicit no interest, allow the fly to drift back well below the fish before lifting off and recasting. Just once in a while, a take-inducing lift with a wet fly will provoke a reaction in peal that seem otherwise wholly uninterested – but the reaction is as likely to be panic as a follow and a positive take, so it is probably as well to reserve this tactic for use as a last resort, when a dead drift has failed completely.

For all the difficulties I have described, the chief problems with sea-trout fishing are that it is highly addictive and that it is somewhat antisocial. It is, without doubt, the most exciting and rewarding form of river flyfishing. Even those who go in pursuit of salmon usually give the sea trout a higher rating, pound for pound, than their primary quarry. But it does make for lost mornings and bleary eyes and, if wives or girl-friends cannot them-selves be addicted to it at an early stage, it is probably best to reserve it for solo or bachelor party holidays.

11
GRAYLING
FISHING

Those of us who fish for grayling often wax lyrical about our sport – about golden autumn days and bright, crisp winter sunshine, and about the fish's beauty, the determination with which she fights and her excellence on the table – and we tend to wonder at other anglers who seem to underestimate and undervalue 'the lady of the stream'.

In truth, though, the grayling's charms can be elusive. Spawning in April or May, she may take up to three months to recover fully and, when caught (usually accidentally) in midsummer, she is likely to be feeble and flaccid, a sorry advertisement for her species. The grayling's prolific nature also militates against her finding favour with trout fishers. Where she lives she tends to thrive, producing myriad offspring, and the capture of an endless succession of four- or five-inch juveniles can be intensely irritating when we are looking for takable trout. It is these factors – along with accusations that she encroaches upon the trouts' food supplies – that have combined to bring down the wrath and opprobium of flyfishers on the poor grayling's head.

And her public relations predicament is helped not at all by the fact that she is at her best when the weather is at its worst. Certainly, we may see an Indian summer in October, with soft, yellow sunlight adding its glow to the mellow hues of the autumn leaves, and we may wake in November or December to find bright sunshine sparkling on frosted trees and meadows. But all too often cold blustery winds and driving rain will persuade all but the hardiest anglers to stay at home, and those who do venture forth are as likely to find their streams and rivers swollen, turbid and unfishable as to find them clear and clean with fish rising obligingly to fine hatches of flies.

There is, in fact, a significant difference in the effective (rather than statutory) length and character of the grayling seasons on chalk streams and spate rivers.

Chalk streams, fed from water tables which gradually subside during the summer, are at their lowest and slowest in September and October, and are usually only fairly temporarily discoloured by rainwater running off the land. But heavy rainfall in October, November and December replenishes the aquifers, and by January the springs feeding the winterbournes will generally have broken. The streams and rivers will be strong and swollen and they may well become stained as they carry away several months' worth of debris accumulated along their banks. Generally speaking, nature herself tends to bring the grayling season on the chalk streams to a close at the end of December or the beginning of January.

Spate rivers, having no water tables but relying instead upon rainwater draining directly off the land, do not show this gradual but sustained change in height and rate of flow. Rather, they rise and fall relatively rapidly in response to showers and storms, maintaining reasonably constant mean levels throughout the year, falling below them in periods of drought and rising above them only quite briefly during and after downpours. So, where grayling thrive in spate rivers – especially in Scotland and in the north of England – it may be possible to fish for them until the end of February, by which time the fish themselves will close the season for us as they come into spawning condition and begin to move onto their redds.

All this being true, it should also be said that fly life on any river is at its least prolific and evident in mid- to late winter, and that for this reason, and because grayling tend to lie deep down in cold weather, bait fishing tends to be far more effective than flyfishing from mid- to late December until the end of February. And, as I explained in the Introduction, I shall not be considering bait fishing in this book – not because I have any moral or other reservations about it (I have not), but because I have very little experience of the techniques involved and think it unwise to pontificate on a subject in which I would be a far better student than a mentor.

So let us consider autumn and early winter flyfishing for grayling, and let us hope for cold days and clear streams – for these are the conditions under which this pretty fish gives of her best and can most ably confound the sceptics who are so quick to denigrate her.

When grayling fishing in the autumn and early winter, let us hope for cold days and clear streams.

It is a mistake to think of grayling fishing simply as a form of autumn or winter trout fishing. Although grayling may be – and often are – caught accidentally when trout are the primary quarry, they are sufficiently different in character and behaviour to merit careful thought and specialized techniques when we set out specifically to catch them.

FISH LOCATION

The first problem posed for the would-be grayling angler lies in actually locating the fish. Unlike brown trout, which are intensely territorial, the grayling is a nomadic creature. Preferring water of even depth and with a steady flow in summer, she generally retreats into deeper water as the temperature drops and by mid-winter will usually have settled deep into the deepest pools. She is a bottom dweller, too, almost always lying close to the river bed, which also makes location difficult, particularly when the water is dark and swollen.

Apart from a tendency to gravitate towards deeper water as the weather gets colder, the grayling's movements are even less predictable than the sea trout's. You may locate fish in a particular pool or run one week and find them gone the next, or convince yourself that a stretch of water is wholly devoid of life and then find it teeming with grayling a few days later.

The only help the grayling gives us lies in the fact that she is innately a shoal fish. You may find individual grayling – sometimes unusually large ones – lurking in deep, dark holes, tucked in beneath steep banks or hiding in inaccessible lies beneath overhanging bushes but, generally speaking if you catch one you may reasonably expect to catch a succession from almost exactly the same place. Grayling also tend to be less shy than trout, but this does not mean that we can be clumsy in the way we approach them.

(As an aside, it is interesting to compare the respective ways in which trout and grayling behave when their suspicions are aroused, perhaps by an angler on the bank. The trout will usually hold its station, perhaps sinking a little in the water, and will become noticeably more alert and vibrant; its body seems to tense and its fins move a great deal faster, almost fluttering. If its suspicions are confirmed, it will dart for cover or dash off at once. The grayling shows none of the physical tension or 'fin fluttering' of the trout, but usually drops warily backwards if it believes that something is amiss. Having done so, she then tends to hold her new position, only turning tail and fleeing if the angler does something crassly obvious, such as standing up on the skyline to cast or walking on upstream along the bank. If trout or grayling show any of these symptoms of nervousness, it is reasonable to assume that we would be wasting our time by continuing to cast to them and we might as well move on and find ourselves another fish to try for.)

FISHING DEEP

The second problem that grayling confront us with is the depth at which they often lie and feed. As is evidenced by their undershot lower jaws, they are very largely bottom feeders, probably taking as much as 90–95 per cent of their food – chiefly shrimps, snails, midge and sedge larvae and the nymphs of various upwinged flies – from or very close to the bottom.

This poses several difficulties – getting our artificial down to the fishes' feeding depth, presenting it realistically slowly in often fast-flowing water, and identifying takes when fishing deep down to fish we will rarely be able to see.

The solution to getting our patterns deep enough is to weight them heavily and to fish them on long leaders. The amount of lead required (and, indeed, the length of the leader) will depend upon the depth of the water to be fished and the force of the current. Neither should be underestimated. Too much weight and too long a leader can usually be compensated for simply by casting a little less far upstream of the fish than we might otherwise have done. Too little weight or too short a leader offer nothing but frustration, making it quite impossible to get the fly down to the fish.

Most of the creatures that grayling feed on at the bottom can be tied with enough lead in them to make them sink quickly, although upwinged nymphs are rather too small and slender to be imitable with a pattern usable in runs of more than moderate depth. And, while they readily lend themselves to weighting and can be deadly on stillwaters, it is difficult to fish an artificial snail or sedge larva slowly enough in rivers to simulate the ponderous, lumbering gait of the naturals.

Several excellent heavy shrimp patterns have been devised and can do great damage amongst shoals of grayling, as can Frank Sawyer's splendid Killer Bug – originally called the Grayling Bug and only renamed when it was found to be just as effective as a taker of trout. As an alternative, my own revoltingly named Wobble-worm, originally designed to resolve the problems of presenting a realistic midge larva imitation to deep-feeding stillwater trout, and very effective for that purpose, has also shown itself to be a useful grayling pattern, especially the beige version fished using the induced-take technique.

As a rule of thumb, our leaders for fishing these heavy patterns should be between twice and three times as long as the depth of the water, depending on the speed of the current. I generally make up these long leaders by securing, say, six feet of 20-pound nylon either directly to the point of the fly line with a needle knot or to a braided butt with a nail knot, then blood-knotting a further, say, four feet of 16-pound nylon to this and finally knotting the front $8\frac{1}{2}$ feet of a knotless tapered leader to the 16-pound nylon. In this case, my leader is $18\frac{1}{2}$ feet long, which will allow me to fish a pool between six and nine feet deep with a moderate flow of water running through it. The overall length of the leader can be increased or decreased by using a longer or shorter 16-pound middle section.

The prospect of casting with long leaders and heavy artificials may seem a daunting one, especially to the novice. 'Wind knots' certainly appear in the nylon much more readily with such equipment than they do when we use more traditional terminal tackle. The key to retaining our sanity is to slow down our casting rate dramatically, and to pause for significantly longer on the back-cast than we normally would in order to make absolutely certain that the fly line and leader are straightening fully in the air behind us before we start the forward cast.

The difficulty of detecting takes is rather less easily resolved. A grayling can take a deep-sunk artificial very gently indeed, causing the nylon on the water's surface to pause only momentarily or, often, not at all. Of course, the top three or four feet of nylon can and should be greased to make it more visible but, even on calm water, nylon will often be difficult to see in flat, grey, autumn and winter light. A better aid to take detection is half an inch of white or brightly coloured wool, well greased with Mucilin and hitched to the butt length of the leader, serving very much like a coarse angler's float. And we must learn to strike at the slightest change in the leader's behaviour, without waiting to ask ourselves whether it was caused by a fish or not. We may waste a little time striking as our artificial bumps into boulders on the bottom or snags on the odd bit of weed, but it is amazing how often we will be rewarded with a solid heave and a well bent rod. The upstream strike, described in Chapter 7, is particularly useful when fishing for deep feeding grayling.

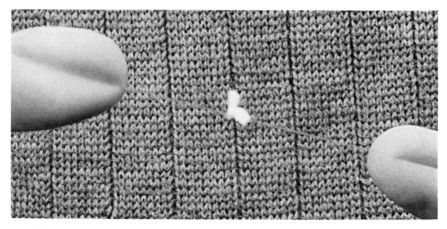

Half an inch of white wool, greased and hitched to the leader, can serve as an efficient float when fishing a leaded nymph to deep-lying grayling.

So, when no fish are showing at the surface (which, despite the claims of some grayling fanatics, will be the majority of the time), we must prospect for them, moving steadily upstream, dropping our weighted shrimps or midge larvae into likely runs or pools. Start at the bottom end of each stretch and fish the water carefully, paying particular attention to deep holes, steep undercut banks, glides beneath overhanging bushes and the slack water above hatches and weirs and adjacent to the boils below them. And, when you catch a fish, remain at the same spot for a while, remembering that grayling are gregarious creatures and that where one has been willing to come to your net her brothers and sisters may well wish to join her on the bank.

THE SURFACE FLY

Unlike trout, grayling tend to rise to surface flies in the coldest, blusteriest and least comfortable weather, provided that the water is clear enough for them to see what is going on above them and that there is something for them to rise to. And, also unlike trout, they almost invariably remain close to the river bed during a hatch, climbing steeply and tipping over almost onto their backs to take the flies and returning to the bottom as soon as they have done so. The rise is distinctive – slightly splashy, often leaving a bubble drifting away on the surface, and very, very quick.

Those who have just spent six months counting to three before hooking trout often find it difficult to come to terms with the speed of response demanded by grayling. A kind friend of mine, the late Harold Horne, used to spend otherwise dull September afternoons casting to shoals of dace on the River Loddon in order to speed up his reactions in preparation for the grayling season to come. I have adopted this training schedule and find it very helpful. There is hardly a stream or river in southern England that does not hold a few shoals of dace, and this quicksilver little fish requires just about the same speed of striking as the grayling does.

THE WET FLY

Grayling also differ from trout in the marked preference they show for attractor flies. Where brown and rainbow trout will often ignore a dry fly that does not approximate quite accurately in size, shape and colour to the naturals upon which they are feeding, grayling can often be taken more readily on pretty, fancy patterns – especially those with a bit of red or yellow or a twist of gold in their make-ups – than they can on a more precise imitation. For myself, I would be quite content to go in pursuit of grayling armed with nothing more than a few Red and Yellow Tags and a few small Wickham's Fancies, to supplement the dry flies I normally use for trout and the Killer Bugs and Wobble-worms with which I search out deep-feeding fish.

One of the courtesies the grayling pays us is that, provided we do not prick her, she will often rise to a dry fly again and again. A grayling having risen to our fly and missed it (or been missed) a couple of times should not persuade us to move on as we might have were we casting to trout. If we have not alarmed her, either by letting her feel the point of the hook or by showing ourselves to her, there is every possibility that she will repeat the attempt. And if she does not, there is every likelihood that one of her companions in the shoal of which she is almost inevitably a part may take up the challenge when she abandons it.

Between deep nymph fishing and dry-fly fishing comes the wet fly – probably the most traditional and widely used method on all grayling rivers apart from the chalk streams, on most of which it is banned.

The techniques used for wet-fly fishing for grayling are much the same as those for trout, and the arguments for and against fishing upstream or across and down are similar too. A surprising number of grayling anglers, particularly in the north country, still fish across and down, probably because it is relatively easy and because it enables them to cover more water than they could by casting upstream. But logic suggests that upstream fishing should be more effective – allowing our flies to sink deeper and pricking far fewer fish – and my own experience tends to confirm this (although I must confess that I have used the downstream method only rarely, having convinced myself of the benefits of fishing upstream at an early stage in my piscatorial life).

Whichever style is chosen, wet fly patterns for grayling can be selected along very much the same lines as dry ones, with imitative or food-suggesting dressings like the Greenwell's Spider and Williams' Favourite working well in low or clear water conditions and rather more gaudy fancy flies such as the Orange and Partridge and the Red Tag taking over as the water becomes more coloured or swollen.

Grayling can be fussy feeders on occasions, ignoring one fancy pattern but taking another very similar one enthusiastically, and their preferences seem to vary from river to river and from day to day. If you are unsure as to what is likely to interest them, it is worth trying a team of two or three, perhaps putting a weighted dressing on the point. And, if you are unfamiliar with a particular water, it always pays to seek informed local advice.

Those who have only ever caught grayling in the summer may be startled by the ferocity with which an autumn or winter fish can fight. Even a $\frac{1}{2}$- or $\frac{3}{4}$-pounder can provide some heart-stopping moments, especially if she gets downstream of you in fast water and then uses her enormous dorsal fin as a paravane, tracking back and forth across the current – which is another argument for casting upstream. Fishing across and down confronts us with the near-inevitability of having to cope with the problems of playing a fish downstream.

As with trout, if grayling are to be released we should be using barbless hooks and they should be freed without being removed from the water. If they are required for the table (and there are few better table fish), they should be dispatched as quickly and humanely as possible.

Grayling fishing is a wonderful sport in its own right and provides a most welcome extension to the trout season. On many waters that hold both trout and grayling, it is possible to fish for as much as eleven months in the year. So let us salute the grayling, rather than castigate her; she is a wonderfully pretty fish and a fine adversary, and she makes a marvellous breakfast.

12

LESSONS

FOR THE

FUTURE

As we saw at the beginning of this book, greatly increased fishing pressure during the past eighty years or so has turned good trout fishing into an extremely valuable commodity. So heavy has fishing pressure become on most southern waters – and, indeed, on many waters elsewhere – that natural populations of trout have had to be supplemented by the introduction of stock fish reared in trout farms. When the need for stocking first became apparent towards the end of the nineteenth century, the requirement was met by the seeding in of brown trout fry, intended to grow on and naturalize, taking their places beside the native stock. This is still done on a small number of carefully managed syndicate waters. But on the most popular and populous rivers increased fishing pressure (and, let it be said, increasing greed on the part of the anglers) persuaded those who managed the waters to stock with substantial numbers of takable fish – with brown trout at first, but subsequently quite often with rainbow trout.

The rights and wrongs of using rainbow trout for the stocking of streams and rivers have been the subject of much debate, and are considered in some detail in Chapter 2. The sad fact is, though, that many of our rivers – including some of the finest – are now little more than running stewponds, stocked with a hotchpotch of farm-reared browns and rainbows, some of them of sizes out of all proportion to the sizes and natures of the waters they occupy, and all of them competing with the native stock for lies and for food.

The trout-farming industry itself, catering both for the table and for the restocking markets, has added to the deterioration of many rivers. Because they live in water, it is easy to forget that trout perform exactly the same bodily functions as all other animals do. But the effluent discharged by a trout farm holding hundreds or thousands of trout can turn the river for quite some distance downstream into little more than an open sewer. And, however careful fish farmers may be, mass escapes do occur, often filling stretches of rivers with thousands of diminutive but voracious rainbows which steal food from the river's rightful inhabitants and can be intensely irritating to flyfishers bent on weightier prey.

I would not wish it to be thought that I am an habitual doom merchant. I am not. The chalk streams still provide marvellous fishing in lovely surroundings, some of it quite readily available to the public, and elsewhere in the country many other rivers are more accessible and better managed than they have ever been. But we must not become complacent. Our watercourses and the fish that live in them are precious assets that must be cherished, and it behoves us all constantly to look for means of conserving them.

It may be that there are lessons to be learnt from the United States. The Americans have a strong tradition of public access to angling waters, born of a belief that what God put into them he put there for the benefit of all men. As a consequence, anybody can fish almost any stream or river in the United States for the price of a state rod licence – just a few dollars a year (although access to many streams is increasingly being controlled by angling clubs). Fisheries management budgets are therefore quite modest, and restocking is generally done with fry and fingerlings, which are expected to grow on to takable sizes. In order that they may be able to to so, American flyfishers are encouraged to fish with barbless hooks and to release the fish they catch, rather than kill them. Substantial stretches of many American trout streams are now designated 'fun fishing' or 'no kill' areas and, elsewhere, there are strict limits on the numbers of fish that anglers may take home, reinforced with slogans like 'Limit your catch; don't catch your limit'. American experience of these policies suggests that trout carefully returned to the water can be re-caught repeatedly, certainly six or eight times or more, and that the use of barbless hooks (essential for the quick and painless release of fish) does not significantly increase the number of trout lost while being played.

Fishing conditions in the United States differ greatly from those in Great Britain. Theirs is a big, sparsely populated country with many lightly fished

141

rivers; ours is a small, densely populated island with relatively few rivers and heavy fishing pressure. I am certain that a blanket public access policy would spell disaster for waters here, but it may be that the active promotion of catch-and-release could enhance trout stocks, reduce the need for restocking and help to provide more interesting fishing. (Incidentally, and in contrast, I am absolutely sure that catch-and-release is a wholly unsuitable management technique for heavily fished small stillwaters – but that is another story.)

While we may have much to learn from the Americans, I think it less likely that New Zealand's policy would be appropriate here, although it may have limited application. There, it is simply illegal to sell trout, which discourages people from killing more than they need for their own purposes. In this country, a great deal of money is tied up in the trout-farming industry, and there is a substantial market for table fish. But there may be advantage in licensing fish farmers, wholesalers and the retailers through whom they deal, and in making the unlicensed sale of trout illegal. If such a law were enforceable, it could help to discourage anglers from killing more fish than they need and from seeking to cover the cost of their sport, or to defray some of that cost, by selling their catches.

Where abstraction and pollution are concerned, considerable progress has been made and many of our rivers are now in better condition than they have been for many years. But, again, we cannot afford to become complacent. We live in a busy, populous industrial and agricultural society, far too few members of which show any real understanding of or concern for the value of our streams and rivers. It is the responsibility of every angler to join and support The Anglers' Co-operative Association (ACA), the only organization which exists solely to prosecute those who pollute angling waters, seeking compensation from them.

It is also important that anglers should ensure that their views are made known to and taken account of by the water authorities. It is easy to forget that the water authorities' essential responsibilities are the treatment and provision of water for industrial and domestic use, sewage disposal and the efficient drainage of land. Although they are also required to make the best use of the leisure facilities afforded by the waters in their areas – and they have done much good work in this field – neither water supply nor drainage is particularly compatible with the good management of rivers for angling purposes. The lowering of water tables by abstraction has seriously reduced river levels in many places. Outdated and inadequate sewage works are frequent polluters of rivers. And, there are still far too many examples of weed stripping (rather than selective cutting) and draconian dredging, with streams and rivers being transformed into featureless canals, all in the interests of efficient land drainage.

142

Finally, there is still room for greatly improved legislation to control pollution by and mass escapes from trout farms. The Danes, who have been farming trout for longer than we have, and more intensively, have learnt the lesson the hard way, with severe damage having been done to several of their major rivers. Regulations covering effluent discharge from trout farms should be no less strict – and no less strictly enforced – than they are for any other potential pollutant, and the penalties for allowing substantial numbers of fish to escape into streams and rivers should be sufficient to encourage tight control and to discourage carelessness.

Every week, the first page of _The Shooting Times and Country Magazine_ carries a quotation from King George VI:

> The wild life of today is not ours to dispose of as we please. We have it in trust. We must account for it to those who come after.

If we want our children and grandchildren to be able to enjoy the wonderful opportunities that we have to fish for trout in lovely streams and rivers throughout the United Kingdom, each one of us has an absolute responsibility to do what he or she can to conserve those waters and their piscine populations and, wherever possible, to enhance them.

REGIONAL

HATCH CHARTS

HOW TO USE THE CHARTS

The charts on the following pages should help river flyfishers to anticipate and identify fly hatches of interest to trout.

Select the chart for the region in which you are fishing.

To choose a sensible artificial, select the month in which you are fishing from the calendar at the left-hand side of the chart; it provides a guide as to when the flies in question most commonly hatch. This should substantially reduce the number of possible options. The time of day at which each fly most often appears should further refine the list and enable you to choose from a relatively small number of sensible artificials.

To identify a natural fly, check its characteristics against the four columns 'Size', 'Body Colour', 'Wing Colour' and 'Number of Tails'. If still in doubt, eliminate alternatives by checking against the calendar and the 'Time of Day' column.

It should be emphasized that one cannot be dogmatic about fly hatches – the naturals can appear earlier or later than their main seasons shown in the calendar. They may be present locally in areas other than those shown in the charts, and they may be absent from some streams and rivers in areas in which the charts suggest they should be present. The charts are no more than a general guide to fly hatches.

REGION: *SOUTH AND SOUTH-EAST ENGLAND*

March	April	May	June	July	August	September	October	Time of Hatch	Body Length (inches)	Body Colour	Wing Colour	No. of Tails
										Natural		

UPWINGED FLIES

Time of Hatch	Body Length (inches)	Body Colour	Wing Colour	No. of Tails
p.m.	$\frac{3}{8}$	Dark Olive	Light Grey	2
Eve'g	$\frac{3}{8}$	Light Olive	Clear	2
p.m.	$\frac{3}{5}$	Cream	Grey	3
Eve'g	$\frac{3}{5}$	White	Clear	3
All Day	$\frac{1}{4}$	Very Dark Olive	Dark Grey	2
All Day	$\frac{1}{4}$	Red-brown	Clear	2
All Day	$\frac{1}{4}$	Mid-olive	Grey	2
All Day	$\frac{1}{4}$	Brown	Clear	2
p.m.	$\frac{1}{4}$	Light Olive	Light Grey	2
Eve'g	$\frac{1}{4}$	Light Brown	Clear	2
p.m.	$\frac{3}{16}$	Cream	Clear	3
Late p.m.	$\frac{3}{8}$	Olive-brown	Dark Grey	3
Eve'g	$\frac{3}{8}$	Red-brown	Clear	3
p.m.	$\frac{1}{4}$	Dark Olive	Mid-grey	2
Eve'g	$\frac{1}{4}$	Dark Brown	Clear	2

SEDGE FLIES

Time of Hatch	Body Length (inches)	Body Colour	Wing Colour	No. of Tails
p.m.	$\frac{3}{8}$	Beige-green	Beige	—
All day	$\frac{1}{2}$	Green	Mottled Brown	—
Eve'g	$\frac{1}{2}$	Brown	Cinnamon	—

STONEFLIES

Time of Hatch	Body Length (inches)	Body Colour	Wing Colour	No. of Tails
All Day	$\frac{3}{8}$	Black	Mottled Brown	2 short

FLAT-WINGED FLIES

Time of Hatch	Body Length (inches)	Body Colour	Wing Colour	No. of Tails
All day	$\frac{1}{4}$	Black	Clear	—
a.m.	$\frac{1}{2}$	Black	Clear	—
Late p.m.	$\frac{1}{8}-\frac{1}{2}$	Various	Clear	—

Probable Species	Suggested Artificials (hook sizes in brackets)			
	Nymph	Wet or Damp Fly	Dry Fly	Spinner
Large Dark Olive Dun Large Dark Olive Spinner	Olive Nymph (12)	GRHE (12)	Rough Olive (14)	Kite's Imperial (14)
Mayfly Spent Gnat	—	—	Grey Wulff (10)	Deerstalker (10 l-s)
Iron Blue Dun Little Claret Spinner	PT Nymph (14)	—	Blue Upright	Houghton Ruby (14)
Medium Olive Dun Medium Olive Spinner	PT Nymph (14)	GRHE (14)	Greenwell's Glory (14)	Lunn's Particular (14)
Pale Watery Dun Pale Watery Spinner	Grey Goose Nymph (14)	—	Ginger Quill (14)	Lunn's Particular (14)
Caenis Dun or Spinner	Grey Goose Nymph (16)	—	Last Hope (18)	Caenis Spinner (16)
Blue-winged Olive Dun Sherry Spinner	PT Nymph (14)	GRHE (14)	B-WO Dun (14)	Sherry Spinner (14)
Small Dark Olive Dun Small Dark Olive Spinner	GRHE Nymph (14)	GRHE (14)	Greenwell's Glory (14)	Lunn's Particular (14)
Grannom			Grannom (12–14)	
Sand Fly			Palmered Sedge (12)	
Cinnamon Sedge			Cinnamon Sedge (12)	
Willow Fly		Alder (Wet) (12)	Alder (Dry) (12)	
Black Gnat			Black Gnat (14)	
Hawthorn Fly			Hawthorn Fly (12)	
Midge	Midge Pupa (14–18)	Adult Midge (14–16)	—	—

NOTE: GRHE = Gold-ribbed Hare's Ear; B-WO = Blue-Winged Olive; PT Nymph = Pheasant Tail Nymph.

147

REGION: *THE NORTH OF ENGLAND*

March	April	May	June	July	August	September	October	Time of Hatch	Body Length (inches)	Body Colour	Wing Colour	No. of Tails
										Natural		

UPWINGED FLIES

Time of Hatch	Body Length (inches)	Body Colour	Wing Colour	No. of Tails
p.m.	$\frac{3}{8}$	Dark Olive	Light Grey	2
Eve'g	$\frac{3}{8}$	Light Olive	Clear	2
Early p.m.	$\frac{1}{2}$	Dark Brown	Mottled Brown	2
p.m.	$\frac{3}{5}$	Cream	Grey	3
Eve'g	$\frac{3}{5}$	White	Clear	3
All Day	$\frac{1}{4}$	Very Dark Olive	Dark Grey	2
All Day	$\frac{1}{4}$	Red-brown	Clear	2
All Day	$\frac{1}{4}$	Medium Olive	Grey	2
p.m.	$\frac{1}{4}$	Brown	Clear	2
Late p.m.	$\frac{3}{8}$	Dark Olive	Dark Grey	2
Eve'g	$\frac{3}{8}$	Mid-brown	Clear	2
p.m.	$\frac{1}{4}$	Light Olive	Light Grey	2
Eve'g	$\frac{1}{4}$	Light Brown	Clear	2
p.m.	$\frac{3}{16}$	Cream	Clear	3
Late p.m.	$\frac{3}{8}$	Olive-brown	Dark Grey	3
Eve'g	$\frac{3}{8}$	Red-Brown	Clear	3
All Day	$\frac{1}{2}$	Light Olive-brown	Mottled Grey	2
p.m.	$\frac{1}{2}$	Brown	Clear	2

SEDGE FLIES

Time of Hatch	Body Length (inches)	Body Colour	Wing Colour	No. of Tails
All Day	$\frac{1}{2}$	Green	Mottled Brown	—
Eve'g	$\frac{1}{2}$	Brown	Cinnamon	—

STONEFLIES

Time of Hatch	Body Length (inches)	Body Colour	Wing Colour	No. of Tails
All Day	$\frac{3}{8}$	Yellow	Dull Olive	2 short
a.m.	$\frac{3}{4}$	Dull Brown	Mottled Brown	2 short

FLAT-WINGED FLIES

Time of Hatch	Body Length (inches)	Body Colour	Wing Colour	No. of Tails
All day	$\frac{3}{8}$	Black	Mottled Brown	2 short
All day	$\frac{1}{4}$	Black	Clear	—
All Day	$\frac{1}{2}$	Black	Clear	—
Late p.m.	$\frac{1}{8} - \frac{1}{2}$	Various	Clear	—

Probable Species	Suggested Artificials (hook sizes in brackets)			
	Nymph	Wet or Damp Fly	Dry Fly	Spinner
Large Dark Olive Dun Large Dark Olive Spinner March Brown	Olive Nymph (12) March Brown Spider (12)	Waterhen Bloa (14) March Brown (Wet) (12)	Rough Olive (12) Kite's Imperial (14)	Kite's Imperial (14)
Mayfly Spent Gnat	—	—	Grey Wulff (10)	Deerstalker (10 l-s)
Iron Blue Dun Little Claret Spinner	Snipe & Purple (14)	Snipe & Purple (14)	Blue Upright (14)	Houghton Ruby (14)
Medium Olive Dun Medium Olive Spinner	PT Nymph (14)	Greenwell's (Wet) (14)	Greenwell's Glory (14)	Lunn's Particular (14)
Olive Upright Dun Yellow Upright Spinner	PT Nymph (14)	Blue Upright (Wet) (14)	Blue Upright (14)	Sherry Spinner (14)
Pale Watery Dun Pale Watery Spinner	Grey Goose Nymph (14)	Poult Bloa (14)	Ginger Quill (14)	Lunn's Particular (14)
Caenis Dun or Spinner	Grey Goose Nymph (16)	—	Last Hope (18)	Caenis Spinner (16)
Blue- winged Olive Dun Sherry Spinner	PT Nymph (14)	Poult Bloa (14)	B-WO Dun (14)	Sherry Spinner (14)
Autumn Dun Great Red Spinner	March Brown Spider (12)	March Brown Spider (12)	Pheasant Tail (14)	Pheasant Tail (14)
Sand Fly	—	—	Palmered Sedge (12)	—
Cinnamon Sedge	—	—	Cinnamon Sedge (12)	—
Yellow Sally	—	Yellow Sally (Wet) (12)	Yellow Sally (12)	—
Large Stonefly	Stonefly Nymph (12)	—	Large Stonefly (10)	—
Willow Fly	—	Alder (Wet) (12)	Alder (Dry) (12)	—
Back Gnat	—	—	Black Gnat (14)	—
Hawthorn Fly	—	—	Hawthorn Fly (12)	—
Midge	Midge Pupa (14–18)	Adult Midge (14–16)	—	—

NOTE: PT Nymph = Pheasant Tail Nymph; B-WO = Blue-Winged Olive.

REGION: *SCOTLAND AND IRELAND*

March	April	May	June	July	August	September	October	Time of Hatch	Body Length (inches)	Body Colour	Wing Colour	No. of Tails
										Natural		
UPWINGED FLIES												
								Early p.m.	$\frac{3}{8}$	Dark Olive	Light Grey	2
								p.m.	$\frac{3}{8}$	Light Olive	Clear	2
								Early p.m.	$\frac{1}{2}$	Dark Brown	Mottled Brown	2
								p.m.	$\frac{3}{5}$	Cream	Grey	3
								Eve'g	$\frac{3}{5}$	White	Clear	3
								All day	$\frac{1}{4}$	Medium Olive	Grey	2
								p.m.	$\frac{1}{4}$	Brown	Clear	2
								Late p.m.	$\frac{3}{8}$	Dark Olive	Dark Grey	2
								Late p.m.	$\frac{3}{8}$	Mid-brown	Clear	2
								a.m. and	$\frac{3}{16}$	Cream	Clear	3
								late p.m.	$\frac{3}{16}$	Cream	Clear	3
								Late p.m.	$\frac{3}{8}$	Olive-brown	Dark Grey	3
								Late p.m.	$\frac{3}{8}$	Red-brown	Clear	3
								All day	$\frac{1}{2}$	Light Olive Brown	Mottled Grey	2
								All day	$\frac{1}{2}$	Brown	Clear	2
SEDGE FLIES												
								All day	$\frac{1}{2}$	Green	Mottled Brown	—
								Late p.m.	$\frac{1}{2}$	Brown	Mottled Brown	—
STONEFLIES												
								All day	$\frac{3}{8}$	Yellow	Dull Olive	2 short
								a.m.	$\frac{3}{4}$	Dull Brown	Mottled Brown	2 short
								All day	$\frac{3}{8}$	Black	Mottled Brown	2 short
FLAT-WINGED FLIES												
								All day	$\frac{1}{4}$	Black	Clear	—
								All day	$\frac{1}{2}$	Black	Clear	—
								Late p.m.	$\frac{1}{8}-\frac{1}{2}$	Various	Clear	—

Probable Species	Suggested Artificials (hook sizes in brackets)			
	Nymph	Wet or Damp Fly	Dry Fly	Spinner
Large Dark Olive Dun Large Dark Olive Spinner	Olive Nymph (12)	Waterhen Bloa (14)	Rough Olive (14)	Kite's Imperial (14)
March Brown	March Brown Spider (12)	March Brown Spider (12)	Kite's Imperial (14)	
Mayfly Dun (not in Scotland) Spent Gnat (not in Scotland)	—	—	Grey Wulff (10)	Deerstalker (10 l-s)
Medium Olive Dun Not in Medium Olive Spinner Ireland	Olive Nymph (14)	Waterhen Bloa (14)	Greenwell's Glory (14)	Lunn's Particular (14)
Olive Upright Yellow Upright Spinner	March Brown Spider (14)	March Brown Spider (14)	Greenwell's Glory (14)	Pheasant Tail (14)
Caenis Not in Caenis Spinner Scotland	Grey Goose Nymph (16)	—	Last Hope (18)	Spent Caenis (16)
Blue-winged Olive Sherry Spinner	Pheasant Tail Nymph (14)	Poult Bloa (14)	Blue-winged Olive Dun (14)	Sherry Spinner (14)
Autumn Dun Great Red Spinner	March Brown Spider (12)	March Brown Spider (12)	Pheasant Tail (14)	Autumn Dun Spinner (14)
Sand Fly	—	—	Palmered Sedge (12)	—
Cinnamon Sedge	—	—	Cinnamon Sedge (12)	—
Yellow Sally	Partridge & Orange (12)	Partridge & Orange (12)	Yellow Sally (12)	—
Large Stonefly	Stonefly Nymph (12)	Partridge & Orange (12)	Large Stonefly (10)	—
Willow Fly	—	Alder (Wet) (12)	Alder (Dry) (12)	—
Black Gnat	—	—	Black Gnat (14)	—
Hawthorn Fly	—	—	Hawthorn Fly (12)	—
Midge	Midge Pupa (14–18)	Adult Midge (14–16)	—	—

151

REGION: *WALES AND THE WEST COUNTRY*

March	April	May	June	July	August	September	October	Time of Hatch	Body Length (inches)	Body Colour	Wing Colour	No. of Tails
— *UPWINGED FLIES*												
█					█	█		p.m.	$\frac{3}{8}$	Dark Olive	Light Grey	2
								Eve'g	$\frac{3}{8}$	Light Olive	Clear	2
█								Early p.m.	$\frac{1}{2}$	Dark Brown	Mottled Brown	2
		█	█	█	█	█		All Day	$\frac{1}{4}$	Very Dark Olive	Dark Grey	2
								All Day	$\frac{1}{4}$	Red-brown	Clear	2
		█	█					All Day	$\frac{1}{4}$	Mid-olive	Grey	2
								All Day	$\frac{1}{4}$	Brown	Clear	2
			█	█	█			p.m.	$\frac{1}{4}$	Light Olive	Light Grey	2
								Eve'g	$\frac{1}{4}$	Light Brown	Clear	2
		█	█					p.m.	$\frac{3}{16}$	Cream	Clear	3
				█	█	█		Late p.m.	$\frac{3}{8}$	Olive-brown	Dark Grey	3
								Eve'g	$\frac{3}{8}$	Red-brown	Clear	3
			█	█	█			All Day	$\frac{1}{2}$	Light Olive-brown	Mottled Grey	2
								p.m.	$\frac{1}{2}$	Brown	Clear	2
		█	█	█				p.m.	$\frac{1}{4}$	Dark Olive	Mid-grey	2
								Eve'g	$\frac{1}{4}$	Dark Brown	Clear	2
— *SEDGE FLIES*												
		█	█	█				All Day	$\frac{1}{2}$	Green	Mottled Brown	—
			█					Late p.m.	$\frac{1}{2}$	Brown	Mottled Brown	—
			█	█	█			p.m.	$\frac{1}{2}$	Brown	Brown	—
— *STONEFLIES*												
		█	█					All Day	$\frac{3}{8}$	Yellow	Dull Olive	2, short
— *FLAT-WINGED FLIES*												
					█	█		All day	$\frac{3}{8}$	Black	Mottled Brown	2, short
		█	█	█	█			All Day	$\frac{1}{4}$	Black	Clear	—
	█							a.m.	$\frac{1}{2}$	Black	Clear	—
		█	█	█	█			Late p.m.	$\frac{1}{8}-\frac{1}{2}$	Various	Clear	—

Natural (spanning the Time of Hatch, Body Length, Body Colour, Wing Colour columns in the header)

Probable Species	Suggested Artificials (hook sizes in brackets)			
	Nymph	Wet or Damp Fly	Dry Fly	Spinner
Large Dark Olive Dun Large Dark Olive Spinner March Brown (Wales only)	Olive Nymph (12) March Brown Spider (12)	GRHE (14) March Brown Spider (12)	Rough Olive (14) Kite's Imperial (14)	Kite's Imperial (14)
Iron Blue Dun Little Claret Spinner	PT Nymph (14)	—	Blue Upright (14)	Houghton Ruby (14)
Medium Olive Dun Medium Olive Spinner	PT Nymph (14)	GRHE (14)	Greenwell's Glory (14)	Lunn's Particular (14)
Pale Watery Dun Pale Watery Spinner	Grey Goose Nymph (14)	—	Ginger Quill (14)	Lunn's Particular (14)
Caenis Dun or Spinner	Grey Goose Nymph (16)	—	Last Hope (18)	Caenis Spinner (16)
Blue-winged Olive Dun Sherry Spinner	PT Nymph (14)	GRHE (14)	B-WO Dun (14)	Sherry Spinner (14)
Autumn Dun Great Red Spinner (Wales only)	March Brown Spider (12)	March Brown Spider (12)	Pheasant Tail (14)	Autumn Spinner (14)
Small Dark Olive Small Dark Olive Spinner	GRHE Nymph (14)	GRHE (14)	Greenwell's Glory (14)	Lunn's Particular (14)
Sand Fly			Palmered Sedge (12)	
Cinnamon Sedge			Cinnamon Sedge (12)	
Welshman's Button			Caperer (12–14)	
Yellow Sally		Yellow Sally (Wet) (12)	Yellow Sally (12)	
Willow Fly Black Gnat Hawthorn Fly	— 	Alder (Wet) (12) — 	Alder (Dry) (12) Black Gnat (14) Hawthorn Fly (12)	
Midge	Midge Pupa (14–18)	Adult Midge (14–16)	—	—

NOTE: GRHE = Gold-ribbed Hare's Ear; B-WO = Blue-winged olive; PT Nymph = Pheasant Tail Nymph.

153

APPENDIX II

FLY DRESSINGS

If there is satisfaction to be had from deceiving a trout with a plausible representation of a natural insect, it is markedly more satisfying if you have dressed that representation yourself. Those who do not tie their own flies often use the excuses that their eyesight is not good enough for so apparently fiddly a task or that they are too clumsy. Neither argument has any validity. Anybody who can thread a line through the rings of a rod and tie a fly to the end of the leader can dress flies that will catch fish.

It would be wrong to suggest that tying one's own flies can save money – except, perhaps, in the long term. Even a simple fly-tying outfit is fairly expensive. But, because a professional is under financial constraints which often compel him or her to use cheap materials and to press every scrap of those materials into service, it is certainly true that with a little practice the amateur should be able to tie a more accurate, serviceable and durable artificial than any that can be bought in a shop.

There is no space here, nor would it be appropriate, to provide a detailed discourse on the craft of fly dressing. In any event, there are plenty of books available on the subject, a few of the best of them being listed in the bibliography. But for the benefit of those who already tie their own flies, or who would learn to do so, there follows a list of dressings for the flies mentioned in the text of this work. Before embarking on the list, a brief explanation of one point is called for.

In discussing the trout's eyesight in Chapter 2, I commented on the way in which a fish sees a natural fly approaching it on the current and pointed to the importance of the appearance of an upwinged fly's wings. This could have been taken to imply that I favour traditional quill-fibre slip wings for artificial upwinged dry flies. In fact, I do not. I believe that a well tied hackle can provide a far more realistic impression of a fly's wings than quill slips can, especially when the pattern is dressed in the 'upside-down' style. So, while I wholeheartedly support the principle of maintaining the purity of the breed – tying flies using the methods and materials specified by their originators – it will be noted that most of my artificial upwinged duns are dressed wingless and 'upside-down'.

ADULT MIDGE (Bob Carnill)

Hook	12–14 Partridge sedge hook (K2B)
Silk	Black
Body	Stripped peacock's eye herl
Thorax	Dark grey rabbit's fur
Wings	Two light-grey cock's hackle points, sloped back
Hackle	Blue dun cock's hackle, sparsely tied

ALDER (DRY) (Anon)

Hook	12–14, up-eyed
Silk	Purple
Body	Peacock herl
Wing	Speckled hen quill slips
Hackle	Black cock's

ALDER (WET) (Charles Kingsley)

Hook	10–12
Silk	Black
Body	Peacock herl
Wing	Speckled hen
Hackle	Black cock's, tied as a beard

ALEXANDRA (originator, uncertain)

Hook	8–12
Silk	Black
Tail	Red ibis substitute
Body	Flat silver tinsel ribbed with fine silver wire
Wing	Peacock sword fibres with red ibis substitute cheeks
Hackle	Black hen's

ANTS – RED AND BLACK (Anon)

Hook	12–14
Silk	Black
Body	Red or black floss silk
Wing	Light buff (or light blue dun) cock's hackle points, sloped back
Hackle	Light buff cock's for the red; black cock's for the black

AUTUMN SPINNER (J. R. Harris)

Hook	12–14, up-eyed
Silk	Claret
Tail	Dark red-brown cock's hackle fibres
Body	Claret seal's fur ribbed with fine gold wire
Hackle	Dark red-brown cock's, tied spent

BLACK AND PEACOCK SPIDER (T. C. Ivens)

Hook	10–14
Silk	Black
Body	Peacock herl
Hackle	Black hen

BLACK GNAT (KNOTTED) (after Freddie Rice)

Hook	12–16 up-eyed
Silk	Black
Body	Black floss silk, or tying silk built up
Hackles	Two black cock's hackles, one at the front of the body, one at the back

BLACK LURE

Hook	8–12 long-shank, tandem
Silk	Black
Bodies	Black chenille ribbed with medium, oval, silver tinsel
Wing	Large bunch of black marabou tied in as a streamer wing

BLUE UPRIGHT (DRY) (R. S. Austin)

Hook	10–14 up-eyed
Silk	Purple
Tail	Medium blue dun hackle fibres
Body	Stripped peacock eye herl
Hackle	Medium blue dun cock's

BLUE UPRIGHT (WET) (after R. S. Austin)

Hook	12–14 down-eyed
Silk	Purple
Tail	Medium blue dun cock's hackle fibres
Body	Stripped peacock's eye herl
Wing	Starling quill slips (or none)
Hackle	Medium blue dun 'henny' cock's

BLUE-WINGED OLIVE (B-WO) DUN (Lapsley)

Hook	14 up-eyed
Silk	Yellow
Tail	Pale blue dun cock's hackle fibres
Body	Tying silk lightly dubbed with 50/50 mix of olive and brown seal's fur
Hackle	Blue dun cock's and red-brown cock's wound together

BUTCHER (Moon and Jewhurst)

Hook	10–12
Silk	Black
Tail	Red ibis substitute
Body	Flat silver tinsel ribbed with fine silver wire
Hackle	Black cock's or hen's

CAENIS SPINNER (Lapsley)

Hook	16 up-eyed
Silk	Yellow
Tails, body and wings	Made from white deer hair, the points making the tail, the body being lashed to the shank of the hook and the bunch of hair then being split in two, tied 'spent' and clipped to $\frac{1}{4}$ inch on each side

CAPERER (Lunn)

Hook	12–14 up-eyed
Silk	Brown
Body	Four or five strands of turkey tail with a 'belt' of yellow-dyed swan's feather
Hackle	One black cock's hackle followed by one red-brown cock's hackle

CINNAMON SEDGE (Anon)

Hook	12
Silk	Brown
Underbody	Gold tinsel
Body hackle	Light-brown cock's, palmered
Wings	Two light-brown cock's hackles, clipped level with the back of the body
Hackle	Light-brown cock's

COCH-Y-BONDU (Anon)

Hook	12–14 up-eyed
Silk	Black
Body	Peacock herl
Hackle	Furnace cock's

DADDY-LONG-LEGS (Lapsley after Fleming-Jones)

Hook	10
Silk	Beige
Body	Bunch of deer hair, extended beyond the bend of the hook and lashed with tying silk
Legs	Six knotted pheasant tail fibres
Wings	Pale blue dun cock's hackle points, sloped back
Hackle	Light-brown cock's

DEERSTALKER (Neil Patterson)

Hook	10 long-shank
Silk	Brown
Tail	Pheasant tail fibres, a full inch long
Body	A bunch of deer hair whipped to the shank, the points just projecting beyond the bend of the hook, ribbed with tying silk and fine silver wire
Hackle	Black cock's wound and trimmed to form a thorax. A large red cock's hackle wound on and then tied 'spent' into two bunches

DUNKELD (Anon)

Hook	8–12
Silk	Black
Tail	Golden pheasant crest feather
Body	Flat gold tinsel ribbed with fine oval gold tinsel
Body hackle	Palmered orange cock's
Wing	Bronze mallard, rolled
Cheek	Jungle cock
Hackle	Hot orange

GINGER QUILL (Anon)

Hook	14
Silk	Brown
Tail	Ginger cock's hackle fibres
Body	Stripped peacock eye feather herl
Hackle	Ginger cock's

GOLD-RIBBED HARE'S EAR (Anon)

Hook	14–16 up-eyed
Silk	Yellow
Tail	Hare's body fur guard hairs
Body	Dark fur from the base of a hare's ear
Rib	Fine, flat gold tinsel
Hackle	Rusty blue dun cock's, or simply some of the longer body hairs picked out at the shoulder

AMERICAN GOLD-RIBBED HARE'S EAR NYMPH (Anon)

Hook	12–14 down-eyed
Silk	Brown
Tail	A few hare's body guard hairs
Abdomen	Hare's body fur ribbed with oval gold tinsel
Thorax	Hare's body fur, picked out to form legs
Wing case	The 'bad' side of a strip of cock pheasant tail fibres

GRANNOM (Lapsley)

Hook	12–14 up-eyed
Silk	Bright green
Body	Hare's ear fur with a bright-green floss silk tag
Wings	Hen pheasant, sloped back
Hackle	Mid-brown cock's

GREENWELL'S GLORY (DRY) (MODIFIED) (Canon Greenwell)

Hook	14 up-eyed
Silk	Primrose, well waxed
Tail	Furnace cock's hackle fibres
Body	Tying silk ribbed with fine gold wire
Hackle	Furnace cock's

GREENWELL'S GLORY (WET) (after Canon Greenwell)

Hook	12–14
Silk	Well waxed yellow tying silk
Body	Tying silk ribbed with fine gold wire
Wings	Starling quill fibre slips
Hackle	Furnace hen

GREENWELL'S SPIDER (after Canon Greenwell)

As for wet Greenwell, but omitting the wings

GREY GOOSE NYMPH (Frank Sawyer)

Hook	12–16 down-eyed
Silk	Fine copper wire
Tail	Grey goose quill fibre points
Underbody	Fine copper wire, humped to form a thorax
Overbody	Grey goose quill fibres twisted with fine copper wire
Wing cases	Grey goose quill fibres

GREY WULFF (Lee Wulff)

Hook	8–14 up-eyed
Silk	Brown
Tail	Bucktail fibres
Body	Grey rabbit fur
Wings	Bucktail tied pointing forward and up, and split in a 'V'
Hackle	Blue dun cock

Note Squirrel tail fibres make an effective alternative to bucktail.

HAWTHORN FLY (Lapsley)

Hook	12 up-eyed
Silk	Black
Body	Black seal's fur
Legs	Two black quill fibres, knotted
Wings	Two medium blue dun cock's hackle points, sloped back
Hackle	Black cock's – sparse

HOUGHTON RUBY (William Lunn)

Hook	16
Silk	Crimson
Tail	White cock's hackle fibres
Body	Red-dyed, red cock's hackle stalk
Wings	Two light blue dun cock's hackle tips, tied spent
Hackle	Red cock's

INVICTA (James Ogden)

Hook	10–14
Silk	Brown
Tail	Golden pheasant crest feather
Body	Yellow seal's fur ribbed with gold wire
Body hackle	Red-brown cock's, palmered
Wings	Hen pheasant tail slips
Hackle	Red-brown cock's and blue jay quill fibres

KILLER BUG (Frank Sawyer)

Hook	8–14 down-eyed
Silk	Beige
Underbody	Fine lead wire
Overbody	Beige darning wool

KITE'S IMPERIAL (Oliver Kite)

Hook	14–16 up-eyed
Silk	Purple
Tail	Brown cock's hackle fibres
Body	Natural heron herl ribbed with fine gold wire
Thorax	Heron herl, doubled and redoubled
Hackle	Honey-dun cock's

LARGE STONEFLY (John Veniard)

Hook	10–14 up-eyed
Silk	Brown
Body	Mixed hare's fur and yellow seal's fur, ribbed with yellow silk
Wings	Hen pheasant quill slips or four dark blue dun cock's hackles, sloped well back
Hackle	Dark grizzle cock's

LAST HOPE (John Goddard)

Hook	18
Silk	Primrose
Tail	Honey-dun cock's hackle fibres
Body	Grey-buff goose quill fibres
Hackle	Dark honey cock's

LUNN'S PARTICULAR (William Lunn)

Hook	14
Silk	Crimson
Tail	Red cock's hackle fibres
Body	Red cock's hackle stalk
Wings	Two medium-blue cock's hackle points, tied spent
Hackle	Red cock's

MARCH BROWN (DRY) (Taff Price)

Hook	12 up-eyed
Silk	Primrose
Tail	Cree cock hackle fibres
Body	Mixed hare's ear and yellow seal's fur ribbed with yellow silk
Wing	Dark hen pheasant quill slips
Hackle	Cree cock

MARCH BROWN SPIDER (Anon)

Hook	12–14 down-eyed
Silk	Brown
Tail	Speckled partridge tail fibres
Body	Dark hare's ear mixed with claret seal's fur, ribbed with yellow silk
Hackle	Grey partridge

MEDICINE (Hugh Falkus)

Hook	3–5
Silk	Black
Body	Painted silver
Wing	Widgeon, teal or brown mallard
Hackle	Blue cock's or hen's

MIDGE PUPA (Anon)

Hook	12–18 down-eyed
Silk	Black
Tail	White cock's hackle fibres cut to $\frac{1}{8}$ inch
Abdomen	Black or dark olive floss silk ribbed with fine silver wire
Thorax	Peacock herl
Breathing filaments	White DRF wool, clipped short

MUDDLER MINNOW Don Gapen)

Hook	6–10 long-shank
Silk	Brown
Tail	Turkey wing quill slips
Body	Gold tinsel
Underwing	A bunch of grey squirrel tail fibres
Overwing	Turkey wing quill slips
Head	Spun deer hair trimmed to shape

OLIVE NYMPH (Lapsley)

Hook	12–14 down-eyed
Silk	Brown
Tail	Three cock pheasant tail fibre points
Abdomen	Dark olive seal's fur ribbed with fine oval gold tinsel
Thorax	Dark olive seal's fur
Wing case	Cock pheasant centre tail fibres

ORANGE PARTRIDGE (Anon)

Hook	12–14 down-eyed
Silk	Hot orange
Body	Orange floss silk
Hackle	Speckled grey partridge, tied sparsely

PALMERED SEDGE (Lapsley)

Hook	10–12
Silk	Brown
Body/wings	Several mid-brown cock's hackles palmered from just round the bend of the hook to just behind the eye and trimmed to a wedge shape
Hackle	Mid-brown cock's

PETER ROSS (Peter Ross)

Hook	10–12
Silk	Black
Tail	Golden pheasant tippet fibres
Body	Rear two-thirds – flat silver tinsel; front third – claret seal's fur; the whole ribbed with fine, oval silver tinsel
Wing	Teal, rolled
Hackle	Black hen's

PHEASANT TAIL (G. E. M. Skues)

Hook	12–14
Silk	Hot orange
Tail	Rusty dun cock's hackle fibres
Body	Ruddy cock pheasant tail fibres ribbed with fine gold wire
Hackle	Rusty dun cock's

163

PHEASANT TAIL NYMPH (Frank Sawyer)

Hook	12–16 down-eyed
Silk	Fine copper wire
Tail	Three cock pheasant tail fibre points
Underbody	Fine copper wire, humped to form a thorax
Overbody	Pheasant tail fibres wound with fine copper wire
Wing case	Cock pheasant tail fibres

POULT BLOA (Anon)

Hook	14–16
Silk	Yellow
Body	Red-brown rabbit's body fur ribbed with fine gold wire
Hackle	Slate-blue grouse under-wing fibres

RED TAG (?Mr Flynn)

Hook	12–16
Silk	Black
Tag	Scarlet wool
Body	Peacock herl
Hackle	Red cock's (dry) or hen's (wet)

ROUGH OLIVE (M. Riesco)

Hook	12–14 up-eyed
Silk	Olive
Tail	Blue dun cock's hackle fibres
Body	Olive seal's fur
Rib	Gold wire
Hackle	Olive badger cock

SECRET WEAPON (Hugh Falkus)

Hooks	Size 8 single with a size 14 or 16 treble in tandem behind it
Silk	Claret
Wing	Brown mallard (sparse)
Hackle	Brown hen's

Note: the fly is baited with a couple of maggots on the front hook.

SHERRY SPINNER (Jim Nice)

Hook	14–18 up-eyed
Silk	Orange
Tails	Light-red cock's hackle fibres
Body	Front half scarlet DFM floss, the whole body then covered with orange DFM floss
Hackles	Blue dun and red cock, wound together

SHRIMP (Lapsley)

Hook	10–12 down-eyed
Silk	Buff
Underbody	Fine lead wire
Body	Brown, grey and pink seal's fur mixed in equal parts
Shell back	Dental dam strip stretched back and forth
Rib	Fine gold wire

SNIPE AND PURPLE (Anon)

Hook	14 down-eyed
Silk	Purple
Body	Built from tying silk
Hackle	Sparsely tied dark snipe

STONEFLY NYMPH (Lapsley)

Hook	12–14 long-shank
Silk	Brown
Tail	Brown cock's hackle fibres
Body	Cock pheasant tail fibres ribbed with gold wire
Abdomen	Peacock herl over a lead wire underbody
Wing case	Cock pheasant tail fibres
Legs	Brown partridge hackle, tied sparsely

SUNK LURE (Hugh Falkus)

Hooks	Two, 8–10, in tandem
Silk	Claret, wound onto hook shanks as body
'Wings'	A bunch of peacock herl and two long blue cock's hackles, tied in at the head, streaming back to the bend of the rearmost hook

165

SURFACE LURE (Hugh Falkus)

Hook	A size 8 single with a size 10 treble in tandem behind it
Body	Cork or goose quill, protruding $\frac{1}{8}$ inch beyond the eye of the front hook and painted silver
Wings (optional)	Two small dark quill feathers

WATERHEN BLOA (Anon)

Hook	14–16 down-eyed
Silk	Yellow
Body	Lightly dubbed mole's fur
Hackle	Feather fibre from the inside of a moorhen's wing.

WHITE MOTH (Lapsley)

Hook	10–12 up-eyed
Silk	Brown
Body	White wool ribbed with brown tying silk
Hackle	Grey partridge, clipped short and very bushy

WICKHAM'S FANCY (?Dr T. C. Wickham)

Hook	14–16 up-eyed
Silk	Brown
Tail	Ginger cock's hackle fibres
Body	Flat gold tinsel
Body hackle	Palmered mid-brown cock's, ribbed with fine gold wire
Wings	Starling quill slips
Hackle	Mid-brown cock's

WILLIAMS' FAVOURITE (Alfred Williams)

Hook	12–16 down-eyed
Silk	Black
Tail	Black cock's hackle fibres (optional)
Body	Black floss silk ribbed with fine silver wire
Hackle	Black cock's (dry) or hen's (wet)

WOBBLE-WORM (Lapsley)

Hook	Partridge sedge hook (K2B), size 12
Silk	Red, green or beige
Head	No. 3 or No. 5 split shot crimped to shank behind eye and painted red, green or beige
Tail	Six strands of red, green or beige marabou, from $\frac{1}{2}$ to 1 inch long
Underbody	Silver lurex for the red version; gold lurex for the beige and green ones
Body	*Very* lightly dubbed red, green or beige seal's fur, ribbed with fine silver wire for the red version and fine gold wire for the beige or green ones.

YELLOW SALLY (WET) (T. E. Pritt)

Hook	14 down-eyed
Silk	Primrose
Body	Dubbed pale-yellow wool
Hackle	Pale-yellow hen

YELLOW SALLY (DRY) (Lapsley)

Hook	14 up-eyed
Silk	Primrose
Tail	White cock's hackle fibres dyed pale yellow
Body	White swan's quill fibre dyed yellow
Hackle	White cock's dyed pale yellow

YELLOW TAG (Anon)

Hook	12–16
Silk	Black
Tag	Yellow wool
Body	Peacock herl
Hackle	Red cock's (dry) or hen's (wet)

THE FLY

FISHER'S KNOTS

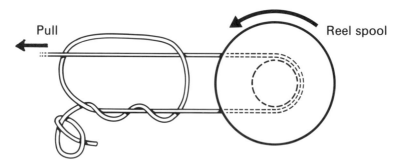

a   A slip knot – for securing backing to a reel.

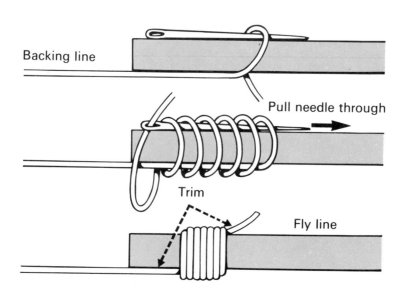

b   A nail knot – for securing fly line to backing.

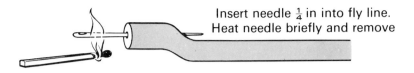

Insert needle $\frac{1}{4}$ in into fly line.
Heat needle briefly and remove

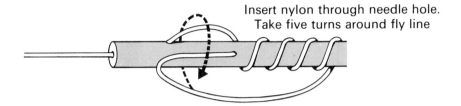

Insert nylon through needle hole.
Take five turns around fly line

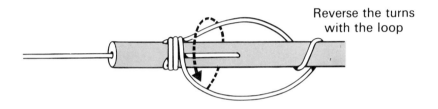

Reverse the turns
with the loop

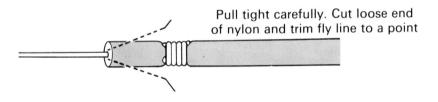

Pull tight carefully. Cut loose end
of nylon and trim fly line to a point

c A needle knot – for securing a length of nylon to a fly line.

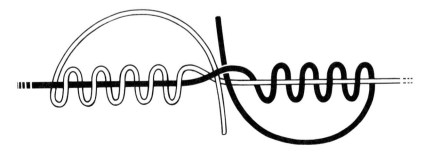

d A blood knot – for joining two lengths of nylon.

169

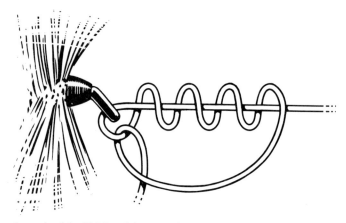

e A tucked half-blood knot – for attaching a fly to a leader.

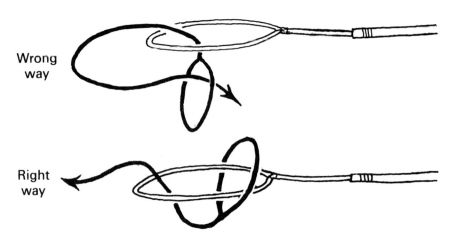

Wrong
way

Right
way

f Loop-to-loop – for joining leader to butt length.

USEFUL

ADDRESSES

INSTRUCTION

The Association of Professional Game Angling Instructors (APGAI), Hon. Secretary: Donald Downs, The Mead, Hosey, Westerham, Kent.

The National Anglers' Council, 11 Cowgate, Peterborough PE1 1LZ (Tel: 0733–54084).

SOCIETIES AND ASSOCIATIONS

The British Field Sports Society (BFSS), 59 Kennington Road, London SE1 7PZ (Tel: 01–928 4742).

The Fly Dressers Guild, Hon. Secretary, H. A. Reid Esq., 18 St Michael's Crescent, Pinner, Middlesex HA5 5LG.

The Grayling Society, Hon. Secretary, Derek Froome Esq., 3 Broom Road, Hale, Altrincham, Cheshire.

The Salmon & Trout Association, Fishmongers' Hall, London EC4R 9EL (Tel: 01–626 3531).

WATER AUTHORITIES AND BOARDS
ENGLAND
Anglian Water Authority, Diploma House, Grammar School Walk, Huntingdon PE18 6NZ (Tel: 0480–56181).

Northumbrian Water Authority, Northumbria House, Regent Centre, Gosforth, Newcastle upon Tyne NE3 3PX (Tel: 0632–843151).

North West Water Authority, Dawson House, Great Sankey, Warrington WA5 3LW (Tel: 092–572 4321).

Severn-Trent Water Authority, Abelson House, 2297 Coventry Road, Sheldon, Birmingham B26 3PU.

Southern Water Authority, Guildbourne House, Worthing, Sussex BN11 1LD (Tel: 0903–205252).

South West Water Authority, 3–5 Barnfield Road, Exeter EX1 1RE (Tel: 0392–50861).

Thames Water Authority, Nugent House, Vastern Road, Reading, Berkshire (Tel: 0734–593366).

Wessex Water Authority, Techno House, Redcliffe Way, Bristol BS1 6NY (Tel: 0272–25491).

Yorkshire Water Authority, West Riding House, 67 Albion Street, Leeds LS1 5AA (Tel: 0532–448201).

NORTHERN IRELAND
Fisheries Division, The Department of Agriculture, Castle Grounds, Stormont, Belfast.

The Foyle Fisheries Commission, 8 Victoria Road, Londonderry, Northern Ireland (Tel: 0504–42100).

The Fisheries Conservation Board for Northern Ireland, 21 Church Street, Portadown, Co. Armagh (Tel: 0762–32276 or 34666).

SCOTLAND
The Department of Agriculture and Fisheries for Scotland, Chesser House, Gorgie Road, Edinburgh EH11 3AW (Tel: 031–443 2529).

WALES

Welsh Water Authority, Cambrian Way, Brecon, Powys (Tel: 0874–3181).

Note For east-central Wales, see also Severn-Trent Water Authority.

REPUBLIC OF IRELAND

The Department of Fisheries and Forestry, Agriculture House, Kildare Street, Dublin 2.

BIBLIOGRAPHY

Some bibliographies are no more than lists of books the author has used in writing his own or to which he has referred in his text. Others are veritable fishing book catalogues. My purpose in compiling this one has been to provide the reader with a reasonably succinct list of good books so that he or she may further explore specific aspects of stream or river flyfishing which may be of particular interest.

BACKGROUND MATERIAL

Barr, David (ed.), *The Haig Guide to Trout Fishing in Britain* (Willow Books, 1983).
Chenevix Trench, Charles, *A History of Angling* (Hart–Davis, MacGibbon, 1974).
Pease, Col. Richard, *The River Keeper* (David & Charles, 1981).
Profumo, David, and Swift, Graham (eds), *The Magic Wheel* (Heinemann, 1985).
Sawyer, Frank, *Keeper of the Stream* (A. & C. Black, 1952; Allen & Unwin, 1985).

THE FISH AND THEIR PERCEPTIONS

Clarke, Brian, and Goddard, John, *The Trout and the Fly* (Benn, 1980).
Frost, W. E., and Brown, M. E., *The Trout* (Collins, 1967; Fontana, 1970).
Sosin, Mark, and Clark, John, *Through the Fish's Eye* (Deutsch, 1976).

ENTOMOLOGY

Field Guide to the Water Life of Britain (Reader's Digest, 1984).
Goddard, John, *Trout Fly Recognition* (A. & C. Black, 1966).
Harris, J. R., *An Angler's Entomology* (Collins, 1952).
Ronalds, Alfred, *A Fly Fisher's Entomology* (Longman Green, 1868).

FLY-FISHING PRACTICE

Edmonds, H. H., and Lee, N. N., *Brook and River Trouting* (privately published, Bradford, 1916).

Falkus, Hugh, *Sea Trout Fishing* (Witherby, 1975).

Fogg, W. S. R., *The Art of the Wet Fly* (A. & C. Black, 1979).

Halford, F. M., *Floating Flies and How to Dress Them* (1886) and *Dry Fly Fishing in Theory and Practice* (1895) (both as modern editions by Barry Shurlock).

Hills, John Waller, *A Summer on the Test* (Hodder & Stoughton, 1924).

Kite, Oliver, *Nymph Fishing in Practice* (Jenkins, 1963).

Leisenring, J. E., and Hidy, V. S., *The Art of Tying the Wet Fly and Fishing the Nymph* (Crown, 1970).

Platts, W. Carter, *Grayling Fishing* (A. & C. Black, 1939).

Pritt, T. E., *North Country Flies* (Low, 1886).

Righyni, Reg, *Grayling* (Macdonald, 1968).

Ritz, Charles, *A Fly Fisher's Life* (Reinhardt, 1972).

Roberts, John, *The Grayling Angler* (Witherby, 1982).

Sawyer, Frank, *Nymphs and the Trout* (A. & C. Black, 1974).

Skues, G. E. M., *The Way of a Trout with a Fly* (A. & C. Black, 1921) and *Nymph Fishing for Chalkstream Trout* (A. & C. Black, 1939).

Stewart, W. C., *The Practical Angler* (A. & C. Black, 1857).

Wilson, Dermot, *Fishing the Dry Fly* (Unwin Hyman, 1987).

FLY TYING

Dawes, Mike, *The Fly Tier's Manual* (Collins, 1985).

Veniard, John, *Fly Dressing Materials* (A. & C. Black, 1977).

Wakeford, Jacqueline, *Fly Tying Techniques* (Benn, 1980).

FOR THE SHEER PLEASURE THEY GIVE

'BB' (ed.), *The Fisherman's Bedside Book* (Eyre & Spottiswoode, 1945).

Hill, W. M., *Fishing Personally* (A. & C. Black, 1986).

Ransome, Arthur, *Rod and Line* (Jonathan Cape, 1929; OUP, 1980).

Voss Bark, Anne (ed.), *West Country Fly Fishing* (Batsford, 1983).

Voss Bark, Conrad, *A Fly on the Water* (Allen & Unwin, 1986).

INDEX